NEVER
TOO LATE

NEVER
TOO LATE

Take Control of Your
Retirement and Your Life

GAIL VAZ-OXLADE

Alex, my baby girl, I love you two bits!
Malcolm, sweetheart, you make my life joyful.
To the best kids a mom could ever ask for.
Thanks for helping me become.

CONTENTS

PART FOUR: PULL THE CHUTE

INTRODUCTION

We live our lives like chapters of a book. There's the kid chapter, the teenage chapter, and eventually the I'm-in-charge chapter. You might have a parenting chapter. You might have a buying-a-home chapter. You most certainly will have a retirement chapter. Now imagine that when you finally turn the pages of that chapter, you see exactly what you want. You've written the scene yourself, and there aren't any surprises. And, best of all, as you're living through all of those other chapters of your life, you're not in the least bit worried about what that last chapter will bring. You know. That last chapter will be one of contentment.

Once upon a time, nobody worried about retirement. You got to 40 or 45 and you died. No problem there. But then life got easier, health care got better, and people started living longer. A lot longer. And a new industry was born: the retirement-planning industry.

I'm not a fan of the retirement-planning industry. While I believe that people do have to plan for when they're no longer working, I've found that the retirement-planning industry has chosen to use fear as its two-by-four, and I'm not impressed. They've created beautiful pictures that people have turned into expectations. And they've used a lot of bafflegab to dazzle us with numbers and make us do things we then scratch our heads at.

What they haven't done is told us HOW. How to save. How to know we'll have enough. How to feel like we're on the right track.

So when my editor, Kate, at HarperCollins, called me up to say that she thought my next book should be on retirement planning, my first response was "What the hell?"

She laughed. Kate is very tolerant of my potty-mouth and instant BIG responses.

"And what will make this book different from all of the other books on retirement planning?" I asked after expressing disbelief with a number of colourful expressions. After all, I'd just done a blog rant on the stupidity with which most Spurts—my word for "spouting experts"—approach retirement planning.

"You'll tell the truth," said Kate.

Hmm. What a concept. A book that tells the truth.

So here I have for you a book about retirement that makes no false promises. There are no hyped-up projections. You won't feel like a loser. And this isn't about Making the Magic Million. Nope. This book is about making sure that when you get to the age—whatever age that may be—where you're no longer slogging it out for money, that you're where YOU want to be. It's about taking control of your future so that when you finally get there you're not surprised at what it looks like. And it's about making sure you know the truth and deal from a place of fact, not fear.

I'll warn you now that not everything I'm going to say will immediately sit well with you. Most people hate the idea of giving anything up in the present for some potential benefit in the future. And there are no special tricks or strategies in this book. Most of this is plain ol' common sense.

There are some very technical areas. This is one of the things that makes most people duck and hide when it comes to planning for the future. But the technical stuff doesn't have to bore you senseless. It's not like you have to memorize it and then take a test. You just have to be aware of it, and know where to find it when you need it, so you can be sure of making an informed decision.

If you've been avoiding the whole issue of planning for your future, and you think your current approach might not really be the best way to have a happy life down the road, then this book is for you. There's no bull, no blather. And you might actually learn a thing or two. You will definitely come away knowing that you are in charge of your retirement and your future. You will know that YOU have the power to make it whatever you decide you want it to be. And you'll know that it's never too late to take control.

Take it slowly. You don't have to finish this sucker in one sitdown. And if your eyes start to glaze over in parts, take a break and come back. I'll still be here.

Your money and your future are too important to ignore. And if you haven't found a good mechanic to guide you through the ins and outs yet—and it would appear most people have not—then you may have to start figuring out how to tune up your money yourself. (And I have some suggestions about finding a money mechanic.)

Most importantly, stop doing nothing. Choosing to stand with your hands in your pockets, whistling a jaunty tune as you cast your eyes around in the hope that no one notices what a dope you're being, is no way to get to where you want to be. For that you have to take action. And for that you need a plan. That's what this book will give you. Concrete steps forward.

And to do that you need to be ready to do this:

1. STOP WORRYING. START SAVING.

How worried are you about retirement? Over the years I've received hundreds and hundreds of letters from people who are at or approaching retirement feeling less than optimistic.

Part of our worry stems from the unrealistic expectations— The Magic Million—established by The Spurts. It seems that doing something isn't enough. We've been told over and over that we have to do the most, regardless of what we have to give up in the rest of our lives so we can accumulate the wads of money some advisor says we'll need.

You can't frickin' win. No matter what you do, by some arbitrary standard, it won't be enough. And so we're left feeling like a bunch of losers. Is it any wonder that so many people throw up their arms and go on vacation?

All the debate about how much you should save is moot in

light of the reality that you just aren't saving. Raising the bar so high that people just stare up at it seems counterproductive to me. Besides, life is expensive. Saving can't be the thing you do to such an extreme that you have no fun while you're getting to the next place in your life. If you've made some past mistakes and need to clean those up, you had your fun and now you must pay for it. But if you're on the straight and narrow, do what you can to have some money for the future—it's really important—but have a life too.

2. BE SENSIBLE.

Are you one of those people who plans to go into retirement with debt? Really? You couldn't get your consumer debt, your car loan, your mortgage paid off while you were working, so you think you'll be able to do so when you're not? While having a small mortgage left isn't the end of the world, having a whopping line of credit or a couple or four credit cards can be the difference between a comfortable retirement and one full of dread.

Or are you one of those people who plan to come to a grinding halt on the work-front at some previously chosen date simply because they want to stop working. Early retirement is a huge dream for many people. And yet they've done very little in the way of asset accumulation or income projection. Y'all do realize that we're living longer, right? At the beginning of 2008, the Stats Man reported that life expectancy had hit 80.4 years, with chicks eking out four years more than dudes. Of course, since you weren't born in 2005, which is the birth year this report is based on, you may croak a little earlier (or later, depending on your family's history). The point I'm trying to make here is that if you retire at 65, you still have 15-plus years to feed, clothe, and house yourself. If you retire earlier, you put even more of a strain on your savings. So you better do some income projections to see just how long the money will last.

Or are you one of the people who haven't, even for a second, considered setting aside some money for the future. You're so busy having a great time right now that the future . . . well . . . it'll be fine, just fine. Heads-up folks. While government pensions may be enough for those people in the lowest income bracket, for many of you it will NOT be enough unless you're prepared to lower your standard of living substantially. If you haven't looked at how much you'll receive from social security, then you should. And if that doesn't motivate you to set aside a little something for the future, I don't know what will.

3. TAKE ACTION.

This book isn't another dust-gatherer, and if you treat it as such, I'll be very disappointed. It's a book of action. It's a book that will help you decide what you want. It's about movement, doing something, taking a step in the right direction. I can't make you save, and if you have no intention of changing anything, don't bother buying this book.

If you are serious about saving a little sumthin' sumthin' so you don't have to cringe every time you hear the word "retirement," this book's for you. If you've been ignoring the long term because you've always felt you couldn't do "enough," this book is for you. And if you're determined to have a balanced, whole life, this book is for you.

Here's the thing: The earlier you start saving for the future, the less money you have to take out of your cash flow because the longer you have the Magic of Compounding on your side. Start early and you can save less. Start later and you'll have to save more. And I'll tell you how much less or more so you'll know just what you need to do.

4. TAKE CONTROL!

Taking control of your retirement and you future isn't as hard as some people think. It's about doing the detail, having some discipline, and being able to prioritize saving some money for the future over yet another television set, new car, or pair of shoes in the present.

Anyone can do it.

I'm going to show you how.

Let's go.

PART
ONE

**FIGURE OUT
WHERE YOU
ARE NOW**

1

CALCULATE YOUR NET WORTH

I have four basic rules for managing money:

1. Don't spend more money than you make.
2. Save something.
3. Get your debt paid off.
4. Mitigate your risks.

Rule #2 is "Save something." But how much should you save? See, that's where the road diverges and people start to get lost. And whenever I'm asked this question, my response is always the same . . . "It depends."

How much you need to save depends on four things:

1. how much you have already saved,
2. how much you want to have,
3. how much time you have, and
4. what kinds of investments/returns you think you'll get.

Getting from here (where you are now) to there (where you want to be) is a matter of measuring the gap and taking steps to fill it. Sounds simple, doesn't it. The devil is in the execution, since there are forks and turns, bumps and jostles that can make what seems like a straight path into something far more daunting.

Each year as I do the media rounds, I am asked, "When should I start contributing to my retirement plan?" For young people, the question implies they have lots of time and can wait. For older individuals, the question is really, "Is it too late for me?"

It is never too late (or too soon) to start saving for your future, no matter how your bottom line reads today. But you do have to know how that bottom line reads. So let's get started.

WHAT YOU OWN VS. WHAT YOU OWE

If you've decided to take control of your retirement and your future, you may be starting from scratch or already well on your way. Depending on how old you are, how much you make, and what you've been doing with your money so far, you may already have a firm foundation from which you can launch your new goal. Or you may have nothing. It doesn't matter. This isn't a race to the finish. This is about knowing where you are now and where you want to be next.

So let's start with where you are. And the way to do that is with a net worth statement. A net worth statement is like a snapshot that shows your financial situation at a particular point in time. In black and white, it tells you how much money would be left if you converted everything you owned to cash and used that cash to pay off everything you owed.

Your net worth statement is a little like a financial report card. You may have been deluding yourself into thinking that you were doing just fine because of that nice pension plan at work and the maxed-out TFSA (tax-free savings account). But if you're also carrying a whopping line of credit and a couple of credit cards with balances, the net worth statement will show you in no uncertain terms where you're really at.

The best thing about a net worth statement is that you can't fool it, unless of course you play loosey goosey with the numbers. There's no rationalizing, no excuses. It's the beginning of an honest and down-to-earth desire to get to where you want to be. And if you're serious about having a little sumthin' sumthin' to see you through retirement, it's the place to start.

If you work through this process and find you have less than you thought, don't get frustrated or sad. Knowing where you are is only the first step. And since it's never too late to get started, working through the process I'm going to give you step by step will help you create a clear picture of what you can achieve. It'll help to get you to where you want to be.

Step 1: Add up what you own
Grab your bank statements, RRSP (registered retirement savings plan) statements, brokerage account statements, TFSA statements, insurance policies and whatever other documents you may have that show what you already own. There's a form on pages 18–19 that you can use to make your notes.

Make a list of the following:

- Cash in your chequing and savings account(s).
- Cash in a money market fund, a TFSA, or government bonds/Treasury bills.
- The cash value of your permanent insurance policy if you have one (not the face value, which is what the policy would pay out; the cash value, which is what you've built up).
- Assets in your RRSP(s).
- The current value of your company pension plan or group RRSP at work.
- Unregistered assets, such as Guaranteed Investment Certificates (GICs), mutual funds, stocks, bonds, or anything else you may own as an investment.
- The current value of your home. Don't guess. Check comparables in your neighbourhood or ask a real estate agent to give you realistic number for what your home would sell for in the current market. Since your home will likely be your biggest asset, you should know what it is worth.
- The current value of your recreational property. (Do not include time-shares since so many have virtually no resale value.)
- The current value of investment property (land, rental units and the like).
- The current value of any other property you own.
- The current black book value of your car or other vehicles you may have (motorcycles, Ski-Doos, boats, and the like). It's important that you use the "black book" value because

you want to be realistic about what you actually have. So
don't guess. Do the research.

- The value of collectibles that could be resold. (Forget about
jewellery or other personal stuff. Those things seldom have
any real resale value and should not be included on your
list.)

- Total what you own. Are you impressed with what you've
managed to accumulate so far? Well, don't go patting yourself on the back just yet.

 ## GAIL'S TIPS: YOUR BIGGEST ASSET

My girlfriend, Victoria, likes to hold "new conversa-
tions" about money. She wants people to think outside
the box, and she gathers them together to talk about
new ways to think about old ideas. When she asked a
group of people what they thought their biggest asset
was, they responded, "My home." You know what, it's
not. While your home may carry the greatest weight
on your balance sheet, your biggest asset is YOU.
It's your ability to earn an income. It's your decision-
making skills. It's your strength of character, your
determination to act, and your willingness to change.

Step 2: Add up what you owe

Make a list of all the money you owe. You'll need your statements to be accurate. Don't guess. Guessing is lazy and lets

you off the hook. Know. Ready to get started? Make a list of the following:

- Mortgage(s).
- Car or other vehicle loans.
- Lines of credit.
- Credit cards (all of them; don't forget the department store and gas cards).
- Investment loans (like the RRSP catch-up loan, but not the mortgage on your investment property, since that's covered above).
- Student loans.
- Buy Now Pay Later plans.
- Pay-advance loans.
- Overdraft (the amount you're into your overdraft for, not the amount you're qualified to use).
- Back taxes.
- Home Buyers' Plan loan from your RRSP. (Hey, you have to pay it back, and even if you owe it to your own RRSP, it's still a liability.)
- Other loans.
- Money owed to family and friends.

Step 3: Calculate your net worth

Subtract what you owe from what you own. That's your net worth.

If you have a positive number, it means you own more than you owe and you're on your way to building up an asset base. If your number is a negative, it means you owe more than you own and you must get busy paying down your debt and building up your savings.

If you're shocked, take a breath. I know looking at the truth can be hard. And seeing where you stand in black and white for the first time can make your stomach churn. But it's okay. You'll be fine. You're doing the right thing by taking these steps now, and you'll be pleasantly surprised at how a little focus and some effort can make a big difference.

Each time you make one of your debts smaller or increase your savings, you're positively affecting your net worth. You'll glory in the progress you make. You'll love the feeling of achievement even as you take small steps towards your goal of having some retirement savings socked away. Your net worth statement can also serve as a deterrent to falling back into old, bad habits. Each time you spend money you haven't yet earned and tip the net worth scale more into negative territory, you'll know you're shooting yourself in the foot.

By regularly updating your net worth statement, you not only check your progress towards individual financial goals, you can also assess how the decisions you make will affect your big picture. Don't underestimate the motivation of tracking your progress in a very concrete way. Your net worth will serve as a reminder of your priorities for when you may need to make adjustments to other parts of your financial life, like your insurance coverage. And it will give you the info you need to estimate your retirement income. Over the months and years, you can chart your financial progress.

Some people update their net worth statements monthly as they pay down debt or build up savings. It becomes a motivator, watching as they move from level to level in achieving their goals. For some, quarterly updates are just fine. But you should do a net worth statement at least once a year to take stock of your overall progress.

Okay, now you have a sense of where you are. The next step is to figure out how you got here and what you have to do to end up where you eventually want to be. For that, you need to figure out your Personal Savings Rate. So that's what we'll do next.

Net Worth Statement

What You Own	$
Cash in account(s)	
Money market fund	
TFSA	
Government bonds/Treasury bills	
Cash value of permanent life insurance policy	
RRSP(s)	
Company pension	
Unregistered assets	
Value of home	
Value of recreational property	
Value of investment property	
Value of other property	
Black book value of vehicles	
Value of saleable collectibles	
Total of What You Own	

What You Owe $

Mortgage(s) _____

Vehicle loans _____

Lines of credit _____

Credit cards _____

Investment loans _____

Student loans _____

Buy Now Pay Later plans _____

Pay-advance loans _____

Overdraft _____

Back taxes _____

Home Buyers' Plan _____

Other loans _____

Owed to family/friends _____

Total of What You Owe _____

Total of What You Own _____

– **What You Owe** _____

= **Your Net Worth** _____

2

DETERMINE YOUR
PERSONAL SAVINGS RATE

Saving is a lost art. You'd think that with all the yada-yada about how important it is to save, what a big deal RRSPs and TFSAs are, and the scant resources we'll have if we count on the government, that we'd all be squirrelling away money for the future at a wicked clip. We're not.

Sure, we know we should save. But what we know we should do and what we actually do are totally different things. Life is expensive, and when all is said and done there just never seems to be any money left to save. The kids' hockey fees are due. The tires have to be replaced on the car. And have you seen how much hydro has gone up? It's a challenge just to get to the end of the month before you get to the end of the money. How the heck are we supposed to find the money to save?

Ahem. That's me clearing my voice as I step up on my soapbox for a minute.

Saving isn't something you do with what you've got left after you've paid all the bills. That's a sure way NOT to save. Hey, there's always a good reason to spend money.

 ## GAIL'S TIPS

Some people don't even know what "saving" is. Hard to believe, but true. Here's what I mean. Most people assume that if they sock away $5,000 a year in an RRSP, they're doing a great job of saving. But if they had to borrow the money to make that RRSP contribution, they haven't saved a nickel until that RRSP loan is paid off. And if they paid themselves first and then promptly upped their line of credit or credit card balances by a similar amount, they haven't saved a cent.

People love to play games, stealing from Peter to pay Paul, and then patting themselves on the back about what good little boys and girls they are. I've worked with heaps of people who have deluded themselves into thinking they are saving because they are building assets. But if they're also increasing how much they owe, they aren't saving squat.

To actually save a dollar you have to take that dollar out of your cash flow. Putting it in a TFSA and then spending it on a credit card doesn't count. You must make the commitment that current expenditures will not exceed current income. You've got to spend less money than you make.

• •

Saving is what you do the minute your money hits the bank. It's a predetermined amount that you set aside every single month because you have a goal and you're dead down-and-determined you're going to achieve that goal.

So let's see how well you're doing.

CALCULATE YOUR PERSONAL SAVINGS RATE

Your Personal Savings Rate (PSR) is a measure of how much money you save out of the money you make. Calculating your PSR lets you know how much you're saving relative to how much you're making. And, as you'll soon see, there are guidelines that can help you decide how much is enough.

While some people talk about your PSR relative to gross income, I don't. You don't make your gross income; you and the Tax Man have to share. I want you to use your net income—your income after taxes—since everything else you will calculate is based on your net income.

Step 1: Figure out your net monthly income

If you don't know exactly how much goes into the bank every month it's time to find out. Grab your bank statements for the past six months. Averages can be deceiving sometimes because there may be periods of the year when you earn far less than at other times. That's why using six months' worth of information is important.

Add up all the deposits you have made. Since transfers between accounts cancel themselves out, you can ignore those. Include all the money that went into your account including your pay, commission, bonuses, support you received, repayment of medical costs or business expenses, and government payments like child, retirement, and disability benefits.

If you belong to a company pension plan or have amounts taken off your paycheque for savings each month, to make this calculation work for you, add those amounts back into your income so they will factor into your savings rate. Look at your last six months' worth of pay stubs. Note any deductions made for Canada Savings Bonds, company pension plans and the like. Add them back into your income. As long as you're saving money for retirement, it has to be added into the calculation.

Some people make a part of their income in cash. If you ignore the cash you make because it goes out as quickly as it came in, your numbers will be off. If you don't know how much you earn in cash each month, you'll have to track forward for a few months to come up with an average.

Once you've totalled up your deposits for the past six months, divide your total by six. That's how much you bring in on average every month.

Step 2: Figure out your monthly spending

Whether you spend money on your credit card, using your debit card, by writing cheques, by accessing your line of credit, or using cash, you need to figure out how much is going out each month. For the purposes of this exercise it doesn't matter what you're spending your money on. We only want to figure out how much you're spending. So add it all up. Your credit card, line of credit, and bank account statements will show you what's been going out. If you've also been spending all the money you earned in cash, you'll need to note those amounts. Remember to divide the six months' worth of numbers by six to get your monthly average.

Step 3: Subtract your monthly spending from your monthly income

This is simple math. Take the amount you earn on average each month and subtract the amount you spend on average each month. That will give you your monthly savings.

So if your average income is $3,600 and your average spending is $3,450, your calculation looks like this:

$3,600 − $3,450 = $150

A positive number means you're saving. But what if you end up with a negative number? That means you're spending more money than you make, so you're going deeper and deeper into debt every month. You may be using credit cards. You may be using a line of credit. You may be using overdraft protection. Rest assured, even if you didn't think there was anything wrong with how you are managing your money, the fact that you've got a negative savings amount should be a very loud wake-up call.

Step 4: Calculate your Personal Savings Rate

Divide your monthly savings by your net monthly income and multiply by 100. So, taking the same example, if your average income is $3,600 a month, and your average spending is $3,450, your PSR calculation would look like this:

$150 ÷ $3,600 = 0.0417 (yes, you need to take it to four decimal places)
0.0417 × 100 = 4.17%
Your PSR is 4.17%

If your average income is $2,900 a month, and your average spending is $3,275, your savings calculation would look like this:

$2,900 − $3,275 = −$375 (oops, is that a negative number?)
−$375 ÷ $2,900 = −0.0129
−0.0129 × 100 = −1.29%
Your PSR is −1.29%

WHAT DO YOU SEE?

If you come up with a positive number it means that you're not spending more than you make and have some savings. Good for you. You have the means to build the pool of cash you'll need to have the retirement life you want to have.

If you spend every penny you make, then your personal savings rate will be zero. You're probably not surprised. You know you aren't saving anything, and now you know why: You have not prioritized saving and you're just coming out even every month.

If you end up with a negative number, you're spending more than you make.

Very often when I show people that they're spending more money than they make, they scratch their heads and ask me "How?"

Really? When you put that dinner on your credit card and didn't pay the balance off in full, it didn't occur to you that you were spending money you didn't have?

Or perhaps you've been dipping into your savings to fill the gap. How long do you think you can keep it up before you've totally depleted your stash of cash?

Hey, you can keep on keeping on, but it's only a matter of time before you hit the wall financially. Wouldn't you rather see the truth and do something positive to paint your picture the way you would like it to be?

Sure there are times when circumstances force us to tap our savings or turn to credit. Medical bills, short stints of unemployment or emergencies can blow up even the most solid plan. But if you're consistently spending more money than you make—and your six months' analysis will tell you this—you're in deep doo-doo.

Spending money you don't have, particularly when you're working a solid week and making good money, means you don't have the good sense God gave a goose. After all, if you can't live within your means when times are good, how will you ever manage when it comes time to hang up your spurs?

If you're determined that saving is important—And you have right? Otherwise why would you have bought this book?—then you are ready to take charge of your retirement and your future. Periodic setbacks are a part of life. Once you've dealt with whatever crap has hit your fan, it'll be up to you to get back on the road to where you want to be next. It won't necessarily be easy. It can be hugely demotivating to have accumulated a bundle of money and then watch it disappear to one of life's cruel turns. But you've got what it takes to beat back the blues, pick up the reins of your life, and move forward. As long as you're built of stern stuff and you're determined, you can get back on track.

Now you know what your PSR is at present. But will it be enough?

Don't worry. I'm not going to leave you with more questions than when you started. In a few pages, you'll get to decide if you're saving enough or if you have to aim higher. You'll know just how much you need to boost your PSR to achieve your goals. And I'll even show you where to look for that extra money so you can achieve the solid goals you've set.

YOU MUST SAVE

If there is a single message I want you to hear it is that YOU MUST SAVE. I know this is a pretty rudimentary statement. But with our savings rate having plummeted, it is the one rule that the majority of people don't follow.

You don't have to start by saving a whack of money. If you've never set a penny aside, making just a small commitment today can make a huge difference to your financial future. So it doesn't matter how little you have to start, the important thing is to start.

One of the questions I am asked most often is this: Why do you tell people to set up a savings account when their money would be better spent paying down their high-cost debt.

Easy. Saving is a habit. It has to be formed.

If the biggest barrier to establishing the savings habit is your sense that you don't make enough to save, think again. Research shows that people with a higher income are no more likely to save than those who make less. Saving isn't just about money. It's about attitude. And without the commitment to having something in the future, the amount of income you earn has very little to do with long-term savings success.

Now that you know your personal savings rate, you'll be able to gauge whether you are on track to achieve your goals by assessing if you are saving enough. We'll talk about that in more detail next. But first, make a note of your PSR here and dog-ear this page.

My Personal Savings Rate is _____**%.**

3

DECIDE IF YOU'LL HAVE ENOUGH

Debates rage about how much money people will need when they retire. Very often the focus of media stories and books on retirement planning is on just how pathetic a life you'll have if you're counting on your government pensions to see you through.

The common thought among those "selling" retirement planning is that if you're banking on the government for your retirement income, you're a fool. One of the reasons they take this stand is that they want to scare the pants off people. Another is that they often don't deal with Your Average Joe. Focused on higher-income Canadians who are far more profitable clients, retirement specialists haven't really taken into account the fact that there are many people who simply don't have a lot of money to save. All they've done with their huge projections of what retirement will cost is scare lower-income Canadians into paralysis or apathy. Some folks hear the numbers and they think to themselves, "Well, I'll never have enough, so what's the point in saving anything. I'm just gonna have as great a life as I can now."

Before you panic and decide your life after work will be one of the seven circles of hell, take a breath. There's no point in giving in to the scare tactics and prophesies of doom. You need to do some work to see for yourself where you'll stand, so we're going to figure out if you'll have enough based on what you're doing right now. Then you'll have to make some decisions about whether or not you like where you are. If you don't, only then will you be motivated to do something different.

Okay, let's get started. First off, you have to figure out where your retirement income will come from.

DETERMINE WHERE YOUR INCOME WILL COME FROM

Your income may come from a number of different sources, including the ones below:

1. **Government retirement benefits:** Old Age Security (OAS), Canada/Quebec Pension Plan (CPP/QPP), Guaranteed Income Supplement (GIS), and the like.
2. **Company pension plan:** Defined contribution or defined benefit plan, group RRSP.
3. **Registered retirement savings:** your RRSP or Registered Retirement Income Fund (RRIF), Life Income Fund (LIF), or Locked-in Retirement Income Fund (LRIF).

4. Non-registered savings: your TFSA, other savings, investment portfolio, home equity, other personal property, insurance cash value . . . almost anything you have that can be turned into money.

If all you will have access to are government benefits because you don't have a company pension plan and you don't plan to save anything while you're working, you'll have to lower your expectations about what retirement life will look like to make sure your money will go as far as you need it to. In all likelihood, you'll be just making ends meet. If you want more than that from your retirement, then you'll have to get busy saving.

You may have a company pension plan, in which case you'll have to figure out how much you'll likely get, as well as how best to manage that sucker. Most people pretty much ignore their company pension plan, often failing even to participate. That's pretty dumb. But hey, now you're done being a dumb bunny and are ready to use all your resources to your advantage, right?

If you think your company pension won't be enough, either because you won't have the years in service to really make it pay or because the payout is less than you feel you'll need, you'll want to do your own saving to top up your nest egg.

You may have no pension plan at work at all, in which case you're on the hook for all the money you'll need to set aside for the future. Hey, welcome to the club. You're among the 11 million Canadians who do not have a company pension plan. Whether you choose to use an RRSP, a

TFSA, an unregistered investment portfolio, or the assets in your home to create a retirement income stream, the ball is in your court.

FIGURE OUT IF GOVERNMENT BENEFITS WILL BE ENOUGH

Almost everyone's going to get a little something from the government. How much depends on a bunch of things like how long you've lived in Canada, whether you contributed to CPP and just how low your income is. If you think what you'll get from the government will be enough, you may be right. Or not.

How much you'll need depends on what YOUR expectations are for retirement. After all, if you're living quite comfortably on $35,000 a year just before you retire, maybe all you'll need during retirement is $24,500, which is 70% of your current income.

I didn't just pull "70%" out of the air. That 70% is what most experts believe a retired person will need to make ends meet. With no travel to and from work, less need for fancy clothes, most of your big purchases made and paid for, and the children gone from your budget, your expenses should come down. And since most defined benefit plans are geared to replace about 70% of your working income, the number has stuck as the rule of thumb for figuring out how much you'll need.

When I quote the 70% Rule, I'm not talking about having a fabulous life, travelling the world, and eating lobster at Sunday brunch. I'm talking about keeping a roof over your head and enough food in your belly.

⏰ GAIL'S TIPS

• •

The higher your income and the lower your expenses, the lower a percentage of your current income you will need during retirement. Let's face it, if you earn $25,000 a year, and your income is just covering your most basic needs now, not much will change when you retire. However if you're making $100,000 a year, and you've got your home paid for, no debt, and a big, fat emergency fund already established, you might be able to live on as little as 50% of your current income when it comes time to twiddle your thumbs.

• •

I'll go into government benefits in more detail in Chapter 11. For now, I just want to make a couple of important points:

1. While we routinely dis our government benefits as being paltry, for some people these benefits are all that stand between eating and being destitute. It may not be much, but it's better than a kick in the teeth.

  For 2008, the maximum OAS benefit was about $497 a month or $5,967 a year. For 2010, it was about $517 a month or $6,200, so you can see how much it increases. Not much. For CPP, the numbers were $880 per month or $10,560 per year for 2008, and $934 or $11,208 for 2010. So you're looking at an annual income of $16,000 to $17,000 in today's dollars if you get the max on both.

2. Do not assume you'll qualify for the maximum government pension benefits at retirement. Find out what you can expect to receive so you can plan accordingly. HRSDC (Human Resources and Skills Development Canada) has a calculator you may find useful. Or you can call them and get the numbers you need.

The maximum OAS benefit is based on being a resident of Canada for 40 years from your 18th birthday. There's more to it and I cover this in detail in Chapter 11, but if you're a new Canadian, you can't assume you're getting the max. The maximum amount for a CPP benefit assumes you earned what's called the average YMPE or average Yearly Maximum Pensionable Earnings—$43,700 for 2008 and $47,200 for 2010—to qualify for the biggest pension. If you didn't, your CPP benefits will be less. And if you haven't paid into CPP for a while, that can screw things up too. Also keep in mind that both CPP and OAS are taxable income.

UNDERSTAND YOUR COMPANY PENSION BENEFITS

If you have a pension plan at work, you're one of the lucky ones. There are only about 10,000 pensions in Canada, and 55% of those are held in the public sector. So while the media likes to bandy about the idea that loads of people have company pension plans, the truth is those people are in the minority. Even worse, many of those who are enrolled (or eligible to enroll) don't understand how their plans work.

● ●

While about 40% of Canadians have access to retirement plans to which their employers will kick in money, it's been estimated that 20% of those who are eligible don't participate. Really? Your employer wants to give you more money and you won't take it? Get thee to the human resources person in your company tomorrow and get signed up. Or are you waiting for me to call you "stupid"?

● ●

Just after my last book, *Debt-Free Forever*, came out, I was talking to my local grocery store owner who told me that, of his 13 full-time staff members, only one—that's right just ONE—was participating in the company pension plan despite the savings-matching program being offered. He said that the number one reason people give is that they "can't be bothered to fill out the paperwork." That may be what they're telling him—leading him to believe they're a bunch of lazy slugs—but I don't believe that's the reason. In my experience, the real reason they don't sign up is that they don't want to have to do without the money that will be moved out of their cash flow and into savings. For some, they are living so close to the line, they simply can't afford to give up the money; that's money they need to buy food. For others, the thought of going without a morning coffee or a movie at the end of the week for the sake of having some money 20, 30, or 40 years in the future just doesn't seem worth it. And herein lies the problem.

While it may be difficult to justify to yourself, your partner or your loving children that NOT spending money you have today means you can have some in the future, that is what you must do if you ever hope to build up some savings for retirement. If you think the future will take care of itself, you're deluding yourself. If you believe your parents, grandparents, or old Aunt Lucy are going to die and leave you a basketful of money, you're nuts. And if you think that the government is going to keep you in the lifestyle to which you have become accustomed, ha ha, the joke's on you!

The only way to have money in the future—for whatever purpose—is to NOT spend it now, plain and simple. And if your company is offering you the option to save and is matching your contributions in any way, you're a fool to ignore this gift. Sure, it's nice to have some extra money in your cash flow for the things you want to do now, but it's not worth the stress and misery of having to live a poor retirement.

If the reason you're not participating in your company pension plan is because you find all the information about your plan bewildering, take heart. Next we're going to go through what you need to know to make your pension plan work for you.

TYPES OF PLANS

Corporate pension plans fall into one of three basic categories: defined benefit plans, defined contribution plans, and group RRSPs.

Defined Benefit Plans

Defined benefit plans (DBPs) incorporate a promise to pay out a regular income calculated according to a predetermined formula. This is the only type of plan with which you know exactly how much you'll receive at retirement.

Defined Contribution Plans

Defined contribution plans (DCPs), also referred to as money purchase plans, define the annual contributions required by the employer (and in many cases by the employee). The size of the pension depends on the amount of money accumulated through contributions and earnings in the plan.

Group RRSPs

Group RRSPs function a lot like regular RRSPs. Your employer runs the plan, and you make contributions by payroll deduction. Since you never see the money, you never miss it.

Some employers match contributions, usually to a maximum of 3% to 5% of earnings, but that's not a given and you should check to see how your group plan works. Keep in mind that if contributions are made by the employer, those contributions are taxable as income to you (but you'll also get a deduction for them), and your total contributions can't exceed the annual maximum RRSP contribution limit.

One of the biggest benefits of a group plan is that you get the tax savings right away, instead of having to wait until you file your tax return for a refund.

• •

You don't have to belong to a group RRSP to reduce the tax withheld from your paycheque when you contribute to an RRSP. Get familiar with Form T1213, which lets you request permission from the Tax Man to have your employer reduce the amount of income tax taken off of your paycheque every month because you know you'll be entitled to a refund.

When you contribute to an individual RRSP, you can clearly demonstrate that you're eligible for a deduction that will reduce your tax bill at the end of the year, so you can trade in your tax refund for more take-home pay. You'll have to fill out Form T1213 and get the Tax Man's approval first, and you'll have to do it every year. While you can do it at any time, the optimum window is in October or November for the following year. Once you're approved, the Tax Man will provide instructions by letter to you, which you then give to your employer, who will adjust your pay for the remainder of the year.

• •

KNOW YOUR PLAN

If you belong to a company pension plan, you need to know how it works. Sticking your benefits book in your bottom drawer because you're too far away from retirement to think about it may be pretty typical, but it's also pretty foolish. That pension plan will be a major asset come retirement. You should know all about it and make sure it's doing all it can while you're working.

Find out what types of plans your company offers. Some plans, like DBPs, offer a guaranteed payout. Others, like DCPs and group RRSPs, don't. You may have a choice in terms of what you can participate in, or your company may have one option, take it or leave it. So will you take it? Or will you leave it and do your own retirement saving and investing?

Is there an eligibility period to belong to your pension plan? While some plans are mandatory, others give you the option to opt out. If you choose to opt in, you may have to wait until you are eligible.

Will you have to make contributions to this plan? Sure, it'll mean less money hitting your bank account, but it'll also mean your savings are automatic and that's a good thing. Find out if you can increase or decrease your contribution as your needs and income change, and if you can make contributions above those required or buy additional pension credits to increase your income during retirement. Ask how your contribution is calculated, whether your employer will also contribute to the plan, and if so, how much.

Find out when the plan "vests." This refers to the time when your employer's contributions officially become yours. This is done to avoid having to pay out itty-bitty pensions to employees who hung around for a nanosecond. Vesting means you've stuck with your employer long enough to have earned the benefits they've set aside for you.

Once you put money into a company pension plan, it has to

be invested to earn a return. If you belong to a defined benefit plan, this is all done for you. But if you're participating in a defined contribution plan or a group RRSP, you have some decisions to make about what investment options to choose. Options are usually limited to those offered by the pension plan operator. Find out how many choices you have and how often you may change your investment mix. Ask about what kinds of returns have been earned on those investment options in previous years. What fees will lop money off the top? If you have to pay commissions, set-up fees or management fees, those will all affect the return in your plan.

Since you may change jobs a time or six before it comes time to retire, make sure you know what will happen to your company plan if you end up leaving your employer. If the pension hasn't vested yet, your contributions will be returned to you. If they have vested, you'll have several options, from leaving the pension in place to transferring the assets to a locked-in retirement account.

KNOW WHAT AFFECTS YOUR PENSION PAYOUT

One of the things you are trying to figure out is whether your pension plan will give you enough money to live on when you retire. Different types of company pensions behave very differently.

If you belong to a defined benefit plan, you can go see your plan administrator to find out how much income you will receive if you stay with the plan until retirement. Of course, that assumes you stick with your current employer to the bitter end. If you don't, you may get substantially less depending on how long you've been in the plan. Defined benefit plans build up over time, chugging along like a car up a hill. Once you reach the magic point at the top, the plan's benefits begin to grow faster and faster, like the car's speed coming down the other side.

If you belong to a defined contribution plan or a group RRSP, your pension payout will depend on how much you and your employer squirrelled away, and how well the investments in your portfolio did, just like with a regular RRSP. In other words, you can take a guess, but there are no guarantees.

Ask what the earliest date you could retire with full benefits will be. Find out if there's a maximum cap on your pension. Also check to see if your pension will be reduced by the amount you receive from CPP so you don't bank on money you won't be getting.

If you're thinking you might want to turn in your shovel early, find out what happens if you choose to retire early. If early retirement is actually being encouraged by your company, make sure you understand how it will affect your short-term (up to age 65) and long-term (after age 65) income. Will your company increase your pension benefits to cover the amount you would have received if you had waited until 65 to claim your CPP benefits?

Or maybe you love your job and want to hang in for an extra year or five. Will that affect your pension?

Since you may be retired almost as long as you were working, inflation will be an issue. Ask if your pension is indexed to provide protection against inflation. If so, when does indexing start?

Indexing is an adjustment of your benefits based on increases in the consumer price index (CPI). Indexing is what protects or partially protects your pension from the ravages of inflation. If your pension offers 100% indexing, and the CPI goes up by 2.5%, so will your pension payments. The idea is to ensure that your pension continues to buy you what it did when you first retired. Not all pensions are indexed at 100%.

If you have a partner, no doubt your buddy will be counting on some of your pension income too. Find out what happens to your pension if you die before you retire. After you retire? If your partner will receive benefits, will they be reduced in any way?

PENSION + RRSP?

For those who are fortunate enough to have a pension plan at work, the question then becomes, "Should I also be contributing to an RRSP?" Well, like most things to do with money, it depends.

The first thing you have to figure out is how good your company pension plan is. Is your plan well funded? Is it well protected? And will it provide what you'll need to retire comfortably? You'll need to go ask your plan administrator some questions before you decide.

If you're a teacher in Canada, you have a terrific pension plan. And if you have a government pension (if you're a civil servant, a police officer, a firefighter or a nurse, for example) and plan to work until you qualify for full benefits, then you'll probably be fine sticking with your pension plan.

Think about when you're likely to retire since most pension plans penalize you heavily for drawing benefits before the normal retirement age. If you think you may want to drop out early, then having some money in an RRSP might be a good idea. But if you're going to sweat it to the very end, you'd be better off maximizing your TFSA every year before looking at an RRSP.

Ask yourself these questions:

- Am I so sure that I'll have this job forever that I am well set for retirement when it comes time to hang up my boots?
- Will my pension be enough, or do I need to have a pool of money for things beyond what my pension will cover? If so, how much do I think I'll need? Am I there yet?
- Are there other things that I could be using these contribution dollars for that would bring me a bigger bang for my buck? This could be anything from educational savings for your daughter to those renovations that you've been longing to do.
- Will a strategy of using a non-RRSP investment portfolio work better for me than investing inside an RRSP? If you're getting a great pension or you're banking on receiving full government benefits, you may decide to do your

investing outside of an RRSP. Why? Well, when you pull money out of an RRSP or RRIF, you take it as "income," which may reduce government benefits that are means-tested. It can also mean you end up pushing yourself into a higher tax bracket, so you end up paying more tax on your pension income.

I'm the girl who constantly shrieks, "Does it work for YOU?" While my basic rules (don't spend more money than you make, save something, get your debt paid off, and plan for the worst) are what I consider the MUST HAVES, the decision to do more, save more, have more later has to be yours.

I often tell people who belong to really good pension plans that they're already hitting their retirement target with their company pension. As long as some crap doesn't come along to throw them off course, that pension will do the trick, so they should have some fun. But it boils down to what is important to YOU.

If you decide you do want to contribute to an RRSP even though you belong to a pension plan at work, know that the calculation is slightly different for you than for folks who don't have a pension plan, since the contribution to the pension plan affects how much you can put in an RRSP.

A pension adjustment (PA) is calculated to equalize, at least somewhat, the benefits received by those who belong to a pension plan and those who don't. The PA reduces the RRSP deduction and represents the amount contributed by an employee and/or employer to an employee account in a defined contribution pension plan or deferred profit sharing plan, or the value of pension benefits accrued during the year in a defined benefit pension plan. In many cases, the PA leaves very little RRSP deduction room remaining, so contributions to an RRSP are moot.

MAKE YOUR OWN PLAN

If you're one of the 11 million working Canadians who does NOT have a pension plan at work, then you're going to be fully responsible for your own retirement savings. Sure you'll get some money from the government when you retire, but for many, that won't be enough.

Welcome to the world of Do-It-Yourself Retirement Planning. You have a number of tools you can use to build your plan, from RRSPs and TFSAs to a wide range of unregistered investments.

Some people are overwhelmed with all the options. The tools look complicated, and like picking up a circular saw for the first time, you may be afraid you'll do more damage than good. But you needn't be afraid. And you don't have to worry that you may have left it too long.

 GAIL'S TIPS

• •

Very often, when people decide to do things differently—pay off their debt, get busy saving—they throw themselves into it whole hog. And just as often, they burn out before they reach their goals. If you want to be successful at this saving thing, you need to find a balance.

Balance is the ability to deal with myriad priorities, giving each just as much attention as it deserves. Balance means not working so hard at accumulating assets that you fail to spend time watching the children play. Balance means weighing the need for future retirement savings with the need for providing your partner, your children, and your friends with fun and exciting experiences in the present. It's about taking care of today and tomorrow. And it's about satisfying your soul while you challenge your intellect.

It can be pretty hard to keep your sense of balance when reality bites—when divorce, widowhood, disability, or unemployment contrives to push you off kilter. "Balance?" you shriek, "How can I have any sense of balance when I'm just barely making it from day to day, paycheque to paycheque?" Ah, yes. Well, that's where the plan comes in.

Balance isn't something that happens. It takes work. It requires that you create a blueprint for your life. And it requires that you take control of the components of your life that you can control, so when you stumble over one of life's bumps in the road you can pick yourself up and move on. It means planning like a pessimist so you can live like an optimist.

• •

If you're determined to take control of your retirement and your future, you can take steps to create the life you want. You've already determined what your personal savings rate is, so you know just how much energy you're putting into your future. You've calculated your net worth: you know exactly where you stand—in black and red—financially. And you have a better sense of how much the government will kick in to help fund your retirement.

Now it's time to figure out what steps you have to take to get from where you are right now to where you want to be 15, 25, 35, or 45 years from now.

You get to decide.

You.

If you choose to do nothing and hope for the best, then when it comes time to step into the next phase of your life you may be disappointed.

If you choose to take steps to plan for the future, no matter how small those steps may initially be, you're likely to have more of what you need to create the life you want. At the very least, you'll have momentum. And momentum goes a long way to getting you from where you are to where you want to be.

And that's what we're going to talk about next.

PART
TWO

**DECIDE
WHERE YOU
WANT TO BE**

4

FORGET WHAT YOU'VE BEEN TAUGHT

If one more person asks me how to make a million dollars so they can retire comfortably, I'll scream. The people who sell retirement planning and the people who typically write about retirement planning have managed to drum into our heads the fact that we're gonna need a bazillion dollars if we ever hope to retire. It's left many of us feeling inadequate. It's left some of us depressed; we know we'll never make it. And it's scared some folks into sticking their heads into the sand and hoping the retirement hunter doesn't come up behind them.

Hey, the hunter's coming. Sticking your head in the sand is not the answer. But neither is The Magic Million that's often tossed about as the Holy Grail of retirement savings. I want you to forget everything you've heard about how much you'll need. Just forget about it. It's irrelevant to you what Jack will need, or how much Jenny will have. The only number that's important is how much YOU will need.

I'm going to help you figure out just that.

The other thing that The Spurts use to put the fear of God into people who are saving for the future is the spectre of inflation. "Inflation" gets bandied about a lot, but most people don't have a clue how it affects them. And you should. Don't worry. I'm not going to ask you to calculate anything. But you should understand what inflation is and how it affects your purchasing power.

KNOW HOW INFLATION WORKS

Imagine that you're selling lemonade. It's a hot day and there's a big demand for a tall, cold glass of what you've got. You can probably charge two bucks a glass and get away with it. Yup, thirsty people won't think twice about shelling out for a little lemony relief. And if you're down to your last glass or two, someone may offer a premium, coughing up an extra 50 cents to grab a glass. So, when supply is low and demand is high, prices jump. Of course, if your next-door neighbours all decide to set up their own lemonade stands, you're going to have to practically give it away to get it off your hands. And if the weather suddenly changes, a cold wind blows the leaves and your customers' thirst away, nobody is going to pay a red cent for your lemonade. What's true for lemonade is also true for money. When there's more money than stuff to buy, prices go up. When there's more stuff than money, prices go down. Inflation is the measurement of the changes in prices of all that stuff.

The Consumer Price Index (CPI) is the way we measure inflation. The CPI is a measure of the rate of price change for goods and services bought by Canadian consumers. It is calculated by comparing the cost of a fixed basket of items that we buy in a particular year. Since the stuff in the basket never changes in terms of quantity or quality, the CPI shows pure price movements.

So what's in the basket? Prices for a whole bunch of stuff including food, shelter, energy, clothing, education, health care, personal care, transportation, recreation, booze, and smokes. It's a big basket, and if you want to know how everything compares, then you look at the whole basket, called the All-items Index. But since most families don't buy everything in the basket every year, the All-items Index—and the inflation rate generally quoted in the media—can be very misleading.

While the overall CPI rose 1.3% in the 12 months ending December 2009, when you look at the smaller groups—like food, transportation, and the like—you get a clearer picture of how our budgets are being hit. In the same time frame, gas prices were up 25.6%. Overall energy prices were up almost 6%, and food prices were up 1.7%. Shelter prices were down 1.7%, primarily because of a drop in the price of natural gas and the decrease in mortgage interest costs. The mortgage interest cost index (yup, that's how specifically the basket can be broken down) fell almost 5% because interest rates had fallen so low during that period.

Canada is a big country, and costs vary widely from one region to another. That's another reason the All-items Index, and the number you hear bandied about, has very little to do with individual Canadians' realities. If you live in the Atlantic provinces and your costs have gone up 3%, you don't give two hoots about the overall CPI number.

DON'T DRIVE YOURSELF NUTS WITH INFLATION

So why do we talk about inflation if there are so many variables and variations? Because inflation affects the purchasing power of our money. If you were trying to figure out how much money you would need in May 1986 to live in May 1996 when you finally retired, wouldn't it be important to know that your dollar would purchase only 74 cents worth of stuff?

And that's why you'll hear all The Spurts talk about how important it is to take inflation into account when you're trying to decide how much money to set aside for the future, and how much you'll really need.

I'm of a slightly different mind. Hey, you can turn yourself inside out trying to figure out how much to save, and how much you'll have, and how much you'll need, but if you don't actually do something, it's all for naught. Sure, inflation will affect your purchasing power. But there's no way to predict it and nothing you can do about it, so turning yourself inside out over inflation is an exercise in frustration. Better to focus on what you CAN save than on how little your money will buy once inflation has taken its bite.

And that's the big problem we're seeing right now. People aren't doing very much. Our savings rate is in the dumper. We've lost hope. We're sure we'll never be able to achieve what The Spurts are telling us we'll need. So we just don't bother.

Stop that!

The only way to take control of your retirement and your future is to DO something. Never mind what you won't have. Focus on what you will have, which will be more than if you turn your back on your future and do nothing.

GET RID OF THE MAGIC NUMBER

Okay, now that you understand inflation, you know it is what it is and being "scared" or "panicking" is pointless. You're also not going to let some Joe who doesn't know squat about you or how you live try to tell you how much you'll need, right?

Perhaps the most damage to our savings motivation has been done by the formulae and massive numbers that have been bandied about by retirement experts and journalists alike. Headlines declare that we'll need a million dollars if we don't belong to a company pension plan. A million dollars? Really? And what do you do if you can't save The Magic Million? Give up?

Projections are just projections. They don't carry any water if the factors on which they are based are no longer true. And how can you "know" what's going to happen in the future?

When I started saving using an RRSP, I was in my very early 20s. At the time, inflation was running at around 12% (yes, really), and one of the first investments I made was a stripped bond paying 14% for 30 years. (A dumb advisor subsequently convinced me to sell for the capital gain back when I was still young and naive and thought those people had my best interests at heart. But I digress.)

All the retirement savings calculators ask you to guess at stuff like your rate of return and inflation. Well, how could we possibly know this since markets change and economic conditions change? We can take a guess, but that's all we're doing. And we should be prepared for the fact that when things do change, so will the projections.

If I had based my retirement planning on the rates of return and inflation of my early investment years, things would look very different from someone starting out now in our current low-interest-rate environment, particularly if we're both very conservative investors.

All this is to say forget about the experts, the projections, the calculators. There is no magic number that will ensure a safe and financially secure retirement. Each of us has a different life, different expectations, and different needs. We must figure out what will work for us as individuals and ignore the tempests in teacups regularly brewed to grab our attention.

Save because you know that you must save if you want to have some money in the future. And save as much as you can. If you start small, so be it. Over time, grow your savings until you are putting away a solid amount every single month. Hey, this isn't rocket science. You'll only have in the future what you don't spend today.

Know that once you jump on the savings bandwagon, it's easy to get carried away. You may even find you want to stop spending money on the things that make life a joy. So when your partner suggests you head off on a lovely vacation together, all you can think about is how much money you'll be "wasting" because it won't be going into your retirement pot.

Give your head a shake. If you put all of your focus on your future, you'll be one miserable puppy to live with.

You have to find the balance between having a great life now, and having enough to keep having a great life when you retire. And knowing how fast your money can grow, given enough time, will give you the confidence to have a life now and plan for the future. So that's what we'll talk about next.

5

UNDERSTAND THE RELATIONSHIP BETWEEN TIME AND MONEY

If there is any magic to be had when it comes to money, it is the magic of how time and compounding work together to make even small amounts of money grow. If you understand how compounding works, you should be telling everybody you know. It doesn't matter if you're 20 or 50, with time you can turn a little into a lot. And it's never too late to start.

Sure, it's great if you know all about the Magic of Compounding when you're 22 and can put decades on your side. But 50-somethings shouldn't throw up their arms in despair because they think they're out of time. If you're 50 now, you retire at 65, and you live to be 85, you've still got a couple of decades for compounding to work its magic.

Let's start at the beginning with some facts.

Fact #1: The longer you invest your money, the more time that money has to grow.

Fact #2: If you are earning a fixed return on your money (read "interest") and there's no chance of capital loss, the longer you invest, the more "compounding" will work for you.

So how much of a difference can time make? Take a look.

THE TALE OF THE TWIN

If you've seen this before, don't go spoiling it for anyone else. It's been used more than a couple of times, but I'd be remiss if I didn't include it because the demonstration is so powerful.

Frank and Jeff are 20-year-old twins who know they need to save for retirement. Frank opens up an RRSP right away, contributes $2,000 a year for 14 years and then stops. His RRSP compounds at 6% a year. Jeff procrastinates, so he doesn't end up opening his RRSP until he's 30. Jeff then contributes $2,000 a year until he's 64. He earns the same return as Frank. They make a bet: Each says his RRSP will be worth more and the loser has to buy dinner.

Who do you think will be paying for dinner when the twins hit 65 and are chowing down on sushi and tapioca?

Name	Contribution	Total Return
Frank	$28,000	$283,400
Jeff	$70,000	$139,200

Even though Jeff contributed more ($70,000) than Frank ($28,000), he ends up with less. Frank's $28,000 will compound to $283,400, compared with Jeff's $70,000, which will compound to $139,200. So Frank ends up contributing $42,000 less to his plan, but ends up with $144,200 more because of the compounding. See the magic now?

KNOW HOW COMPOUNDING WORKS

So what exactly is "compounding?" Compounding is the process of generating a return on an asset's reinvested earnings. In the simplest terms, it's the interest you earn on the interest you earned.

Let's say Susie invested $15,000 last year at 5.5%. She earned $825 in interest.

 GAIL'S TIPS

• •

Whenever you want to multiply by a percentage, you multiply by the percentage number and divide by 100. So 5.5% is actually 5.5 divided by 100, which makes the math look like this:

15,000 x 5.5 = 82,500
82,500 ÷ 100 = 825

• •

So now Susie has $15,825. Susie decides to keep her money invested for another year. If she earns the same rate of 5.5%, her investment will grow to $16,695 by the end of the second year.

15,825 × 5.5 = 87,038
87,038 ÷ 100 = 870.38, which we'll round down to 870
15,825 + 870 = 16,695

Because Susie reinvested the interest she earned in the first year, it works with the original investment to earn more return—$45 more ($870 versus $825). "Peanuts!" you say. "Hardly worth the effort." What effort? Susie didn't have to lift a finger to earn that $45. On top of which, that $45 now has the opportunity to earn even more return. In another year, Susie's $15,000 investment will have earned $918 in interest and will be worth $17,613.

16,695 × 5.5 = 91,823
91,823 ÷ 100 = 918.23, which we'll round down to 918
16,695 + 918 = 17,613

That's the Magic of Compounding in action.

Compounding only works if you add your return to your original investment. Some people have no patience. They also have a hard time deferring gratification. So if Susie earns $825 in interest on her investment, and sees it as "found money," she'll rush right out and spend it. Susie's justification: I didn't have to do anything for that money so it's like a gift. By spending it, Susie just robbed herself of the Magic of Compounding.

Okay, so compounding makes your investments grow because every dollar you earn in return goes on to earn more money.

 GAIL'S TIPS

• •

Here's a rule you need to know about if you're trying to figure out how your money will grow; it's called the Rule of 72. It's a simple way to determine how long it will take for your investment to double. It's often used with people who are investing in interest-bearing options like saving accounts or GICs, usually to make them feel small and stupid because their return is low and it's taking sooo looong for their money to grow. But it's a good rule and you should know it. It goes like this:

The number 72 divided by the return on your investment will give you the number of years it'll take for your money to double in value.

So, if you're getting 5.5% return on a GIC, then the formula would look like this:

72 ÷ 5.5 = 13 years

This formula is actually a little off, and gets more "off" as the rate of return increases, particularly when you're looking at returns of 20% plus. (You wish, right?) But it's handy, particularly for the math-challenged. And it can be used backwards too: Want to double your money in six years? Divide 6 into 72 to find that you'll need to earn a return of about 12%.

• •

MORE TIME MEANS MORE MONEY

If Susie can grow her $15,000 to $17,613 in just three years, imagine if she had 20, 30, or 40 years. The more time you put on your side, the greater the growth you'll experience in your investment portfolio. For the following example, I'm using an investment of $1,000 a year, which earns an average annual return of 5%. To keep it simple, we'll say the money is growing on a tax-deferred basis, in either an RRSP or a TFSA.

Total Deposits Value	Amount Saved	Grows To
If you're 50 and have 15 years to save	$15,000	$22,657
If you're 40 and have 25 years to save	$25,000	$50,113
If you're 30 and have 35 years to save	$35,000	$94,836
If you're 20 and have 45 years to save	$45,000	$167,685

This is the growth on just $1,000 deposited at the start of the year. One thousand dollars, that's all. That's $83 and change a month. If you are 30 and you start right now, that $1,000 a year will net you almost $100,000 in savings over 35 years.

You can do it. It's that easy. And the earlier you start the better off you'll be. Given only 15 years, the contributions compound to grow by 151%. Put more time on your side and your result will be more inspiring. With 35 years to compound, $1,000 a year will grow by 271%. And if you're a wise young person and start early, well, the sky's the limit, eh?

Don't believe me? There are loads of calculators all over the web. Find one, pop in your figures, and see for yourself how great saving can be!

If you really want to blow your mind, look at what happens to the numbers when your return goes up by just 1%, from 5% to 6%:

Total Deposits	Value @ 5%	Value @ 6%
15 years to save $15,000	$22,657	$24,673
25 years to save $25,000	$50,113	$58,156
35 years to save $35,000	$94,836	$118,121
45 years to save $45,000	$167,685	$225,508

With less time (15 years), the difference in growth is nothing to write home about. You'll make another $2,016 over 15 years. Big whoop, right?

But look what happens if you have 35 years to go: You'll have an extra $23,285 just for having worked hard to find an extra 1% return on your money. And if you've got 45 years to go? Tada . . . $57,823.

Yah, Gail, but who has the foresight to start investing when they're 20? Well, you don't have to start when you're 20 . . . compounding doesn't care about your age, just about how much time you have until you need to spend the money. So if you wait until you're 45 to start and work until you're 70, you've still got 25 years.

All this is to say that the more time you have, the more growth you can achieve without having to take on loads of risk to get super-high returns. Just a small increase in your investments' performance can make a huge difference with enough time. And by starting to save from the moment you start earning some money, time can work wonders to get you to where you want to be.

Yah, Gail, but I'm no spring chicken. Does that mean I'm screwed? Hey, if you want to throw your arms up and say, "Why bother, there's no point," nothing I say is going to make a whit of difference. But if you want to be in control of your retirement and your future, know that it's never too late.

If you're 50 and retirement seems to be rushing towards you like a speeding truck, do something. Find a way to cut just $5 a day from your spending. Drop coffee, lunch at work, and those magazines you pick up at the checkout when you're grocery shopping. Skip a take-out meal or night out and enjoy some good ol' home cookin'. Cancel the premium cable or bundle your home phone, Internet, and cell bills. Do whatever it takes. Invest that five bucks a day—just five bucks—using an automatic monthly savings plan in either an RRSP or TFSA, and in 20 years at a return of 5%, you'll have over $61,655.

Deciding what you want and laying a plan to achieve your goal are the first steps. Then you must act. Do something. Cut out coffee and save that money. Trim your grocery budget and save that money. Get another job and save that money. You're the boss. You're in charge. It's your life. Where are you going with it?

GET STARTED SAVING

Inertia can be your enemy or your friend. If you haven't been doing much so far, and it feels easier to just keep on doing nothing, know that inertia has got you. But shake free of the inaction, take a step towards putting the Magic of Compounding on your side, and you'll turn inertia into a positive thing: Your body in motion will remain in motion. You'll keep on keeping on with saving.

No doubt the very next question that will pop to mind is this: So how much should I be saving? Well, that's the next thing we're going to figure out. Here we go . . .

6

FIGURE OUT HOW MUCH YOU'RE GOING TO SAVE

Okay, you've decided to bite the bullet and start saving. Good for you. Or you've been saving all along and now you're serious about figuring out whether you're on the right track. Or perhaps you have a pension plan at work, and you're now trying to decide if you should supplement that with additional savings.

How much you need to set aside depends on a bunch of things:

- how much you've already saved (or have socked away in your company pension plan),
- how much you think you'll need (will you have a simple retirement or do you want to be able to gaily gad about?),
- the returns you're earning on your investments, and
- how much time you have to save.

Let's start by looking at how your age affects how much you need to save.

SO HOW MUCH IS ENOUGH?

It's been estimated that if you start saving in your early 20s, you need only put away about 6% of your net income to end up with enough to maintain the lifestyle you enjoyed before you retired. You can pace yourself. You have time working for you, and you can adjust your stride as you go to deal with whatever you may encounter. You're in it for the long haul.

 GAIL'S TIPS

Your percentage amount won't change over time, although the amount you are saving will as your income increases. So once you start saving at 22, putting away your 6% diligently every year, you'll never have to increase your percentage amount. Starting early not only means more time for your money to compound, it also means more cash flow later.

Wait until you're in your 30s to start saving and the "save 10%" rule takes on a very special meaning . . . it's the least you can do. Sure, you don't have as much time, but you're still fine. You'll have to pick up the pace or decide that a little less later on is fine.

Wait until you're in your 40s and you'll have to run faster, socking away 18% of your income to have what you'll need.

Start in your 50s and know that you're either going to have to work a little longer or a lot harder to have enough.

You may have started saving a while ago but are unsure what your PSR is because you were just squirrelling away whatever you could. Hey, I applaud you for being smart enough to have started saving. But now you need to factor in the amount you've already saved to decide how much you should continue saving.

 GAIL'S TIPS

I believe you should be saving as much as you can comfortably afford to save, without squeezing your budget so tight it squeaks. Yes, you have to have a life. Yes, you deserve at least some of things you're working so hard for. But I don't want to put an upper limit in a dollar amount on how much you should be saving since each person has to figure out their own personal money set-point. I will say that erring on the side of having more savings isn't a bad thing unless it means you're miserable (or making other people in your life miserable) because of your rabid savings habit.

So how do you do that? Simple. If you're in your 20s, you know you need to be saving 6% of your net income. Check back to the PSR you calculated in Chapter 2. Are you hitting

6%? If so, good. If not we'll look at ways to ratchet it up in the next chapter.

If you're 30 or older, it's time to have a look back at your net worth statement that you calculated in Chapter 1. If you've hit your 30s and your net worth is the equivalent of one year's worth of salary, you can assume you are hitting the mark and stick to saving 6% of your income. If your net worth is less than that, you should ramp up your savings to 10%.

If you've hit your 40s and your net worth is the equivalent of five years' worth of salary, you can assume you are hitting the mark and stick to saving 6% of your income. If you're only at three years' worth of salary, assume you were saving 10%. If it's less than that, increase your savings rate to 18%.

If you've hit your 50s, you should have about eight times your salary accumulated. If you don't, you'll have to up your savings rate to as much as 25% or 30%, delay your retirement, or reconcile yourself to a much simpler lifestyle when you do retire. With less time for compounding to do its magic, most of your retirement income will be coming directly from what you manage to sock away between now and when you do stop working. You should aim to have 11 times your salary socked away by the time you hit age 60.

 **GAIL'S TIPS**

All this assumes you do not belong to a defined benefit plan. If you do, your pension benefit payout will be a percentage of your final earnings just before you retire. Find out from your pension administrator what your projected payout is. If you're quite happy living on the amount your pension will pay out, you're set. You don't have to save another penny. But if you think you want to have a little more socked away, you'll need to save more. How much more? Well, that depends on how much you want to have. You could just max out your TFSA every year and that'd give you a nice cushion.

Even if you do belong to a DBP, you may feel uncomfortable banking on those benefits 100%. Why? Well, in the winter of 2009, the Certified General Accountants Association of Canada reviewed the state of Canada's private pensions and found that the vast majority—over 90%—were in a deficit position, meaning they didn't have all the money they should have to pay out all the benefits they were promising.

• •

Okay, time to go back to the end of Chapter 2, where you wrote down your Personal Savings Rate.

Now that you know what percent you should be saving, it's time to see how close you are.

My personal savings rate is _____ %
I should be saving _____ %
My gap is _____ %

Take your gap percentage and multiply it by your average

monthly income to see how much you need to be saving in actual dollars.

If your income is $4,300 a month, and your gap is 7%, your calculation would look like this:

$$4,300 \times 7 = 30,100$$
$$30,100 \div 100 = 301$$

So you would have to increase your savings by $301 a month to have enough.

Do your calculations, and write down how much you need to add to your savings each month.

I need to increase my savings by $_____ .

If you don't think you can come up with whatever number you arrived at today, don't panic. And for heaven's sake, don't give up. You've come so far already. I'm going to talk about how you can find the money to save in Part 3, so keep going.

Before we go looking for the actual dollars you'll need to stash away for the future, I want you to figure out what's going to keep you motivated to save. Goals are like children: Whichever is shouting loudest tends to get the most attention. It's pretty difficult to stay focused on Quiet Rebecca Retirement when you're decades away and Loud Hanna House is shouting at you. So let's figure out what turns your crank, and what'll keep it turning.

IF YOU'RE IN YOUR 20s OR 30s

If you pick up just about any book on retirement planning you'll see the standard advice:

- Think about what you want from your retirement.
- Run the numbers.
- Create a plan and stick to it.

Here's the problem: this advice has little or no practical value for you if you're young and just getting started. I know when I was 20 years old I couldn't even imagine what my life was going to be like when I was 40, never mind when I turned 60. So how could I focus on a goal that was so far away? But I knew I would need money. And I knew the only way to have money is to make money and not spend it all.

Trying to decide how much you'll likely need at retirement takes some future gazing, and the further you are from retirement, the foggier your crystal ball will be. If you're in your 20s or 30s, you likely have no idea how much you'll be making just before you retire, so how could you possibly know how much you'll need when you finally do turn in your shovel? This is one reason why people don't get busy saving when they are young. Unable to set a concrete goal, saving feels a little like running on a hamster wheel: You're working really hard at it, but you just don't know if you're making any real progress.

Take heart. Doing the right thing consistently will get you to where you want to be. Or at least in the general neighbourhood. Doing nothing, on the other hand, is no answer at all. It's just giving in to the vagaries of uncertainty.

If you're a long way from retirement, despite not being able to tell how much you'll need, or what's going to change between now and then, you're actually in the best position since you have heaps of time on your side. Because of the Magic of Compounding, early savers can behave a lot less desperately than those who are a nanosecond away from needing a pile of money and having nothing saved. Hunting down an elephant-sized return won't be half as important, because you have time doing most of the work for you. If you can sock away $100 a month—or $1,200 a year—in an RRSP and earn 5.5% on your money on average over 40 years, you'll have put away $48,000, which will have grown to almost $172,934.

The big message isn't that you have to figure out how much you're going to need, it's that you have to get into the habit of saving. And that means not spending every red cent you make no matter how great the temptation. It means giving a nod to the idea that money not spent now is money you'll have in the future. And it requires that you be conscious about what you're doing with your money, as opposed to just letting it slip through your fingers.

The struggle to balance building retirement assets for tomorrow against today's very real demands for cash means that often saving is pushed to the side. Oops. There goes saving, hidden behind "not enough money," "making ends meet," and "paying off student loans." While all these may be valid—yes, you want to make paying off your student loans a priority—they can't be used as "excuses" for not saving. Let's face it, we're great at coming up with excuses for not saving. Saving takes more discipline than many people want to exert. But if you want to balance today's needs with tomorrow's, then you've got to stop making excuses and start saving.

If you think you can put off saving because later you'll be earning way more money and will have more money to save, it's time to wake up and smell the coffee. Would you rather save 6% starting now, or 18% later when you also have kids to raise, a mortgage to pay, and only heaven knows what other competing priorities?

Treat your savings like a marathon instead of a sprint and you'll achieve three things.

1. You can take less out of your cash flow to meet your goals.
2. You'll put time on your side, so compounding can do its magic.
3. You'll have to think about it less.

Saving will be so automatic for you that you'll barely have to consider it. You'll save because it's what you always do.

 GAIL'S TIPS

. . . .

People who don't save think they have a great excuse for not doing so.

There are the folks who say, "I'm paying off credit card bills." Sure, carrying debt means mortgaging your future income. But if you can't find a way to get your debt paid off and save money for the future, you're not trying hard enough. Whether you get a second job, a third job, or a better job, you have to find a way to make more money. Or you can trim your spending back to the bone for a few years to get your debt gone and then ramp up your savings. But you've got to start saving. For as long as you're not saving, you'll continue not to save. That's the law of inertia. You have to make a conscious and deliberate effort to get unstuck.

Then there are the folks who say, "I have to look good." Paying a premium to flaunt a famous name while not saving for the future? You're a fool. If you're defining yourself by the brands that some starlet who makes 100 times what you make wears, then you're a pathetic fool. Expensive brands are no substitute for a solid financial future. A car is a means of transportation, not a reflection of your identity or success. I scratch my head at young people starting out who think they should be driving a $50,000 luxury vehicle. Even if you buy one second-hand, they are more expensive to maintain and insure. I guess the big question is this: Is it more important to look rich or be rich?

Then there's the "Everyone else has stuff. I want stuff too," whine. I can't believe the number of people who not only spend money they haven't made yet, but then need a bigger home to keep all that STUFF. Sell the stuff, trim your housing costs, and get busy saving. If impulse control is your problem, the easiest way to not spend—and therefore to have money to save—is to stay out of stores. If you're shopping as entertainment, find something else to do. Never go into a store without a list. And pay cash, or have the cash ready to pay off the credit card if you're disciplined enough to use them as a tool and not as a financial bridge.

And the granddaddy of reasons to not save: "I don't have anything left to save." Sometimes this isn't an excuse, it's a truth. If that's the case, then you're already pretty good at making do on less, and relying solely on government benefits when it comes time to retire will continue that trend. But more often than not the very people who cry too poor to save are wasting money. You've seen me peek into people's refrigerators. Inevitably when there's no food in the house, the spending analysis shows gobs of money spent in restaurants and on take-out. If you want to have some money to save, make a menu for the week, shop with a grocery list, stock your fridge with fresh food, and use your freezer to save time on busy nights or when you're just too tired to cook.

• •

SAVE BECAUSE IT'S THE RIGHT THING TO DO

If you're just starting off in your life, retirement is likely the last thing on your mind. But just because you can't imagine hanging up your spurs when you've only just got on the horse doesn't mean you shouldn't be saving something.

So the big question is, are you ready to start setting aside a small amount of money now so you have a good pile of money later?

Hey, it's your choice. You can take control now or keep pro-crastinating: $50 a month now or $2,500 a month when the reality of retirement finally throws the coffee in your face. So, what's it gonna be?

IF YOU'RE IN YOUR 40s

It's one of life's big jokes that as we earn more money we seem to have less money at our disposal. Like a gas expanding to fill a container, our expenses grow as our incomes increase. We want to have a family. We need a bigger house. It's time to trade the compact for a minivan.

And then comes the message that if you don't start paying attention, cat food's gonna be too good for you. Oyyy! Well, if you've arrived at your 40s with little saved, you do have some catching up to do. But there is no point in beating yourself up or playing the "I shoulda" game: "Gosh I shoulda saved more when I was younger." You are where you are and now you're going to take some steps to get to where you want to be next.

Imagine Your Retirement

If you look at the way retirement is painted, you might come to believe that your retirement will be vastly different from the life you now lead. With the banter about what you'll want from your retirement raising the standard on fun to unre-alistic levels, people think that if they don't have The Magic Million, they'll be way off the mark and will live horrible lives of deprivation and misery.

Think again. If you don't have wanderlust now, in all likeli-hood travel will play a relatively small part in your retirement future. And if your idea of a fabulous afternoon is chasing a ball around a golf course, that's pretty much what you'll want to do later.

There are stories of people who completely revamp their lives when they stop working, embracing changes that would make a 20-year-old's head spin. But that's not the case for most people. Yes, you are going to have to find activities to take up the time you've spent busting your butt to get to retirement. But in all likelihood it will be the simple pleasures that make your life lovely to live. Think sleeping in. Think having time to spend with friends you were always too busy to see. Think time with the grandkids or with your church pals.

When the Stats Man looked at how physically active Canadians are in retirement, there weren't a lot of surprises. About 26% of men younger than 54 are physically active and about 27% of men 65 to 74 are physically active. See, not much changes when retirement arrives. Women do tend to slow down a bit more with 22% of younger women versus 17% of older women being physically active. While you're unlikely to head off to the senior Olympics, you likely won't become a boozehound either. Only 48% of seniors drink regularly, compared to 67% of young 'uns.

All this is to say that your life is unlikely to change dramatically when you retire. Dreams of antique hunting, world travel, and hours spent on a sailboat, the wind tossing your silver hair back from your sun-kissed face, are highly overblown. You're much more likely to spend more time reading, sprucing up the garden, and having a cuppa with your neighbours.

Okay, so retirement isn't going to look like an ad from a

financial-services company. What will it look like? Have you given it even a moment's thought? Most people haven't. They're so busy rushing through life, getting the bills paid, making the presentation at work, hauling the kids to hockey or to university campus tours, that they never think about what they want from the chapter of their lives that's just around the corner.

Find Your Motivation

The reason financial-services companies spend millions of dollars trying to paint you a picture of what the future may look like, is to help you find the motivation that will stop you spending today so you can have something you want in the future. Sure, all they want is your money—your dollars invested in their hands so they can earn a nice profit—but the tactic they're using has merit.

It's pretty hard for most people to not spend money. Spending comes naturally. Saving is a different story. And with hugely competing demands on your cash flow, saving is easy to slide to the back burner.

While some people come to saving naturally—for them it's a habit like brushing their teeth—if you're not one of those people then you need to take a page from the advertising world's book and come up with an image that turns your crank. You need to visualize something meaningful for YOU for your future. You have to paint a picture that will give you something to focus on.

You might be single-minded in your picture painting. Or you may choose to use a collage of images to create the feel you hope to achieve in retirement. However you choose to do it, the mere act of focusing on what the future may hold for you will help you clarify the need to save. If you won't want to sell your home and downsize immediately, you'll need some cash to see you through your early non-working years. Or maybe you won't have early non-working years, opting instead to use the skills you developed at work to build your own small business during your early "retirement" years so you can feed your travel bug.

The most important part of this exercise is to be true to what YOU want. Never mind the images the media create for us, or the dreams and desires your friends are expressing. You need to be working towards something that really lights YOUR fire for the weight of your motivation to wrestle spending to the mat. The second-most important thing: talking to your life partner about what he or she may think life will be like in the future.

Ignore the "all or nothing" message shouted at you. You do not have to forgo all the fun. Remember, the idea is to balance today's needs with tomorrow's. When you're painting your picture, don't make your plan so grand that you end up defeating yourself with unrealistic expectations. Start small, grow your image over time, and keep your perspective.

If you haven't yet started saving, coming up with 18% may seem like a very big challenge. Don't let that deter you from taking action. While you may not be able to find all the money to save right now, at least now you know what you should be saving. You have a goal. And it's a goal based on your needs, not some stupid number pulled out of the air. Take it one step at a time. Stay focused. I'll help you to find ways to save more in Part 3.

IF YOU'RE IN YOUR 50s

Let's take a minute to talk about how you feel about being in your 50s and not having a pot to pee in. Retirement with no money set aside can feel like a nightmare about to happen. Hey, you can let your fear paralyze you and make all those worst-case scenarios running through your head come true, or you can use that fear to focus your efforts and accomplish as much as possible in the time you've got left.

Yes, you're terrified. I get that. So now you have to make some choices. Remember, YOU get to decide when you retire, which means you can give yourself more time by choosing to retire later.

It's important that you acknowledge how you're feeling about the next chapter of your life. If you simply push those emotions away, the fear you're feeling will paralyze you. By dealing with the emotions, you can become proactive about when you'll retire. You can even practise how you'll live during retirement to get a taste of the future.

Deal with the Emotions

If only you'd started to save even a little bit when you first started working. It sucks. I know. But focusing on what you've done wrong, or what you should have done, or what could have been different if only, isn't going to get you anywhere except to Miseryville. You can smack yourself upside the head, wallow, and wail. None of it will do you a bit of good. You might as well save your energy for dealing with the problem.

We all make mistakes. I've made some doozies, and I've spent some time trying to figure out what the hell I was thinking. It's amazing how the mistakes we've made can take on a life of their own, growing to unbelievable sizes in our minds, weighing us down with "if-only's" and "I-wish-I-hadda's."

Some people just can't forgive themselves. They feel so stupid, so guilty, so riddled with remorse that they refuse to cut themselves any slack. They must pay by being miserable. But where you are now is not where you must stay. And not every mistake we make is as big as it appears to us: With a front-and-centre view of what we've done wrong, and unlimited repeats running in our minds, it's easy to forget the things that are right in our lives and focus only on the messes we may have made.

We are all human. We all make mistakes. If we learn from them, then those mistakes are worth something. If we walk around with our bag of mistakes—ever growing—hung from our necks, we become so weighed down that our energy and passion are sapped.

Perhaps the biggest step is to stop chasing the feelings of self-loathing around our heads by acknowledging the mistake and its implication. Say it out loud to another body or write it out where you can see it in black and white so that you're holding yourself accountable. "When I bought Nortel at $70, I had not done enough research and was operating on the assumption that what goes down must go up. I was wrong. I won't buy any more investments on speculation." Never mind how it looks to the person to whom you are "confessing" or how hard it is to admit the mistake you made. What is important is that you own up to the mistake, acknowledge what you did wrong, and say what's going to be different.

Now the tough part. Say this out loud: "I forgive myself. I made a mistake. I'll make more. But I'm also getting smarter by the day. And for that I am very proud."

Give yourself a hug to celebrate your new freedom. It's never too late and today is the day you focus positively on the future. Take control and step back into the light so you can see where you're going, rather than being mired in the misery and darkness of your "mistake." Off we go now . . .

How Do You Feel About Retirement?

Money is only one of the things you're worried about. You're also wondering what the hell you're going to do with yourself when they hand you your hat and kick you out the door. After all, you've defined yourself in part by what you've been doing for the past 30 years. All your friends are at work. Work is why you get up in the morning.

Or not. Maybe you can't wait for the whistle to blow so you can head out the door, your bundle over your shoulder, whistling all the way. You're anticipating sleeping in, having afternoon tea with your best friend, and driving the country taking pictures and making new memories. The only fly in the ointment is the money you haven't saved. Now that you're almost out of time, you've got a sinking feeling in your stomach.

Aside from not stashing away some cash for the future, waiting until you're within a hair's breadth of retirement to develop the interests you can carry into retirement often means you have a less satisfying retirement. It is now, while you are still working, that you must find the balance in your life that will let you focus on some of the things you enjoy doing. Those with the foresight to be physically active, develop a hobby or three, and volunteer are often far happier in retirement than the people who come to a grinding halt at work and then scramble to find stuff to do with their new-found freedom. The need to feel useful, the desire to maintain social contacts, and the drive to be stimulated intellectually don't evaporate once you head out to pasture.

If you've been doing your due diligence, saving for retirement and planning for what your life will be like next, you may just need to tweak the plan a bit as you get closer to the date. If you haven't done sweet-diddly-squat, your 50s are really your final kick at the can. Once you hit your 60s, there simply isn't enough time left to save enough to make a difference unless you keep working for at least another 10 to 15 years.

The good news is that most of your larger expenses—the kids, your mortgage, your student loans—should be all but gone by this point. And since you're also likely in your peak earning years, you may have lots of money to work with.

Or you may not. If you're one of the people who has been barely covering your butt most of your working life, the idea of moving into retirement with not a lot saved may be keeping you up at night. Relax. Having lived frugally most of your life, you're an old hand at making your dollar go as far as it can. That'll come in handy.

Choose Your Retirement Date

Don't forget that YOU get to say when you retire. Just because the normal retirement age is 65 doesn't mean that's when you have to pack your suitcase and head to Sleepy Pines. You can choose to keep working well past 65 if it suits you—building up a bigger stash of cash and reducing the number of years you have to live on a retirement income.

 GAIL'S TIPS

• •

Up until 2011, for every year you delay taking your Canada Pension Plan past age 65, the amount you could receive increases by 0.5% per month up to 30%. New legislation set to phase in between 2011 and 2016 will increase the amount the CPP will go up if you wait. For each year you wait, you'll get an extra 8.4% (instead of 6% under the old rules). So if you hang on until 70, your monthly CPP cheque will be 42% higher than it would be at age 65.

• •

Health and money are the two biggest drivers when it comes to setting a retirement date. Not having enough money means extending your working career. Not having good health often means moving into retirement because your body just can't take another day of dragging itself to work.

In 2006, over 300,000 Canadians between the ages of 55 and 64—so, pre-retirement age—had an average income of less than $7,000 because of a disability. That's a lot of people who very likely had planned on being able to earn a healthy income, but were derailed by their bodies.

Assuming you have your health—hey, you're eating well,

getting some exercise, and have banned all stress from your life, right?—the key to making the transition to retirement a smooth one will be to not just let it happen to you. Falling into retirement because you haven't really thought about it, because you've turned 65, or because you've been laid off and can't imagine getting another job shouldn't be how you make this transition. If you want to be happy, you have to have a sense of some control over the process. YOU have to be in charge.

Practise Living on Your Retirement Income

One of the best ways to prepare for a significant change in your life like retirement is by playing Let's Pretend. Practising living in your future retirement circumstances lets you develop a feel for what it will be like and get ready to make the adjustments necessary. By simulating your retirement life, you not only see how you will feel, you'll get some experience with what you'll have to do to make it work.

First, figure out how much you'll have as a monthly income during retirement. If you're on track with your savings, you can use 70% of your current income as your guideline. Not confident about your savings? Then fall back to the benefits you know you're guaranteed to receive like OAS, CPP, and whatever pension you may have from work, but only if it is guaranteed.

Once you come up with the figure you're going to have to live on, you'd actually have to live on that money, cutting back where necessary to make the money come out even. Impossible? Well, now you at least know how much extra you'll need, which will lead to how much you must save to have the income you'll need in retirement.

 GAIL'S TIPS

• •

Living the retirement experience is important because people operate with a set of myths that may have no bearing on their reality. Perhaps because we've had it drummed into our heads that we'll need only 70% of what we were living on, people think their costs will immediately go down in retirement. Research shows that's not true for some folks, at least for the first few years. If you have a load of pent-up experiences—travel, home improvements, or a slew of new hobbies—the early days of retirement can prove more costly than you anticipated and throw your budget out of whack.

• •

By living the experience, you'll come up with some new info you may have overlooked. Most people never even think about remitting income tax since it's automatically deducted from their paycheques. But when you retire, you're responsible for making sure your taxes get to the Tax Man on time. Will it be better for your cash flow to do it monthly or quarterly? How much will you have to remit? (Don't guess. Use an online tax calculator to figure this out.) And what exactly do you have to pay tax on when you're retired? (Again, don't guess. Ask your accountant or financial advisor for help.)

Ditto your insurance needs. With no mortgage (you did plan to retire without a mortgage, right?) and no dependent children, you may not need as much life insurance. But you may need long-term care insurance or to replace your health care benefits that used to be covered at work.

Playing Let's Pretend also gives you an opportunity to think about what you want from your retirement. You get to visualize what retirement life will be like for you. Will you spend time volunteering? Will you work part-time? And is it important to retire by a specific date or are you willing to delay retirement so you can save more—and live more comfortably—later on?

Let's Pretend helps you avoid the miscalculations and misrepresentations most people make when they make retirement plans. Do the planning. Live the experience, even for a couple of months. That'll give you a concrete way of gaining a clear sense of what life will be like so you can focus on making good decisions about how you'll do it when the time comes to execute your plan.

 GAIL'S TIPS

• •

While you're practising living on your retirement income, you'll likely be spending only 70% of your current income, leaving 30% that you can use to boost your savings. You may even find that having started this exercise, the experience of living on less isn't so bad, leaving you with more money to set aside to build up an extra stash of cash for the future. And since you're going to have to learn to live on less anyway, the practise might be enough to form some new, very beneficial habits.

• •

Okay, so now you know where you stand and what you still must do to have the retirement you want. And you've stopped beating yourself up for what you haven't done yet. You're in a better place. You're taking charge of your retirement savings and your future. It won't be easy. And sometimes you'll get very frustrated. That's life. At least now you know, so you can do something about how the next part of your life turns out. Or not. It's up to you.

IF YOU'RE IN YOUR 60s

You're part of a growing crowd of folks who are headed into new territory. Once upon a time when people retired they didn't do much. As the baby boomers move into their 60s and 70s, they are redefining "retirement." You're not happy to just go away quietly like many of your parents did, being incorporated into your children's busy households or shuffling off to a nursing home. Nope. You're a whole new breed of retiree: independent, self-directed, and determined to create new experiences for yourself.

Not surprising, really, since your generation could just as easily be called the Generation of New Things. You were the first to have television and fast food. Your world changed at a pace never seen before, and you kept up. Technology bloomed. Travel became routine. Food went from meat-and-potatoes to cilantro and lemongrass, pesto and prosciutto, sushi and sashimi. You've gotten used to doing things differently and you're not about to stop.

If you're among the 60-somethings, you're almost out of time when it comes to saving unless you decide to defer your retirement for at least 10 years. It's time to focus on the immediate future; take a good hard look at where your money will be coming from and how you're going to spend it.

When will you retire? The earlier you retire, the more you'll need to get you through retirement. According to the Stats Man, our average life expectancy continues to go up and the gap between men and women is closing. So if you're planning to retire at 60 and stay on this mortal coil until you're 82, you'll need enough money to get you through 22 years of not working. The longer you put off your retirement, the more you can accumulate before you trade in your workboots for a pair of really comfy shoes, and—just as important—the less time that money has to last.

Will you work part-time during retirement? If you do, you'll be able to supplement your pension with money you earn. This is a growing trend, as we recognize that work ain't all that bad after all. In 2005, over 20% of retirees were working.

How much will you need/want to spend? This is the really BIG question. If you're spending $60,000 a year now, in all likelihood you're going to need a little more than $20,000 a year to make ends meet.

Some people arbitrarily pick a goal for how much money they think they'll need. That's where The Magic Million came from. It was a dart thrown in the dark. And it's no truer for the guy who is currently living on $250,000 a year than for the guy living on $25,000. Guessing is fine if you're 20 and just starting out. After all, life is going to throw you a huge number of curveballs before you actually get to take off the glove. But if you're in your 60s, it's time to stop guessing, focus, and do some serious groundwork. The last thing you want to do is get to retirement only to find out that you have enough money to last until next Tuesday. We'll talk more about this in Part 4.

So now you're thinking differently. You know you have to save and you're finally motivated to do things differently. Now you just have to figure out how to squeeze every last penny you can from your budget while still having a life and some fun, so you can achieve your retirement goals. Hey, you can do it. I know you can. Loads of people find the way to balance their retirement savings with their other priorities and you can too. Now it's time to look at how you do that.

PART
THREE

**START!
NOW!**

7

FIND THE MONEY

Hey, you're still here. Wow! That must mean you've found your focus and are ready to do something about your future. Great! Now it's time to find the money. There's no magic to this part. You've got to figure out your natural tendencies when it comes to saving. You've got to find the money to save. And if you're behind the eight ball, you've got to squeeze every penny you can from your budget so you have something to put to work for the future.

This part of the book is going to call for a big dose of honesty and an even bigger dose of hard work. Are you ready?

HOW COMMITTED ARE YOU?
There are lots of people who say they want to save but don't have the tenacity to stick it out. They're what I call Saving Wussies. Lots of talk, no action. Lots of whining about how

hard life is, no commitment to doing WHATEVER it takes to make saving a reality. And then there are the people, the Saving Demons, who won't spend a penny that's not in the budget because they are hell-bent on getting to their goal. Do you know what you are?

It is important to know how committed you are to this process so you can take your personality into account when choosing how to go about saving. We're all different. We see life in unique ways. And our temptations and our rewards drive us down diverse paths. There is no one right way. There is only the way that works for each of us as individuals. So, how committed are you?

- **Not at all committed.** You love to shop. You can't save a penny. You think you should. Or you know you should. Or you wish you could. But you're not going to suffer one minute of discomfort. You're never going to delay your gratification or say no to yourself. Money is for spending, and that's what you keep doing. You know what? It's your money. Spend it all. Just remember you can't go whining to your friends, family, or me, when you don't have two red cents to rub together.

Since you're not at all committed to saving, and can't get the impulse monkey off your back, you could help your case of "got-it-spend-it" by locking your savings up so you just can't get at them. Set up an automatic deduction from your regular bank account to an RRSP, TFSA, or other account and have the money moved before you get a chance to spend it. Make sure you don't have access to that money . . . make it be "work" for you to get to it so you aren't tempted to tap the account every time you see something new and sparkly that catches your fancy. You're working on the Out-of-sight-out-of-mind Savings Program.

The very fact that you're reading this book means you want things to be different. I applaud you for that. It can be tough to work against your own nature. But that's where your intellect comes in. It is your emotions that drive you to spend. And it'll be your intellect that lets you overcome those urges to spend all your money by finding ways to hide it from yourself. If you can take a logical approach to what you must do for your future, you'll win. And you'll have all my admiration because I know how hard this can be.

- **Somewhat committed.** You've been told you should be saving and you think that it's probably a good idea. It's just that stuff keeps cropping up FORCING you to spend your savings. The car breaks down, your son's hockey fees come due, your daughter needs a dress for the dance, your husband wants a new TV, your wife is desperate to redo the kitchen. The list goes on and on and on. You squirrel away a few bucks and then, BAM, something knocks the money out of the savings account and into your pocket. Oops!

I get that you find saving frustrating because something always seems to crop up. Just when you think you're on a roll, disaster strikes and all your hard effort seems to have been for naught. Don't beat yourself up. Don't give in to the frustration.

Know that you must take steps to protect your efforts from the erosion you constantly seem to experience.

First, you need to keep some money accessible for emergencies. Make two pools of savings: one that you can touch when caca happens, and one that is untouchable.

Second, lock that untouchable money up where temptation can't steal it. Think: three- to five-year GICs and government bonds. You shouldn't use anything too liquid (i.e., easy to sell like a money market fund) because the temptation will be to cash out and spend the money. Now, if you run into trouble, you can't default to using your long-term savings because they're not available. You'll have to get creative and find another solution. Which you will. Because you're smart. And because you must.

- **Very committed.** You get it. You're determined to save. You may not have a lot to start with, but that's not going to stop you. You've set up an automatic debit from your chequing account to a savings account, RRSP, or TFSA to accumulate your goal amount. And every six months, you increase the amount you're saving by 10%, 15%, or 20%, so you keep growing your savings. You're learning all about retirement savings plans, and you're determined to take full advantage of the tax savings they offer. Ditto educational savings accounts, investing, and whatever else will help you reach your goals.

Look how smart you are. I'm impressed. And I think you have a great future ahead of you. Your ability to defer your gratification, to prioritize, to see what needs to be done is admirable. You know you can have it all, just not all at the same time. You've got what it takes to make anything you want for yourself.

- **Passionately committed.** You're so committed to reaching your goal that you've actually taken an extra job and are directing all the money you're making from that job to your RRSP or TFSA. You're a fiend when it comes to finding ways to cut costs, and every penny you "save" using coupons or shopping on sale goes immediately into your savings account. Yup, you don't save $10 without applying that $10 to your savings! Woohoo. You're a train and everyone better get out of your way, because you are determined to reach your goal.

 GAIL'S TIPS

. . . .

While most often I have to encourage people to save, sometimes I have to encourage people not to focus on saving quite so much. I know "financial freedom" is all the rage, but I've watched people sacrifice their present to try to achieve a financial goal without really ever understanding what they are giving up. If you're just accumulating a crapload of money in the bank, what's that all about? Balancing today's needs and wants with tomorrow's is the key to managing money well. Yes, you need to save so that you have options. But if you prioritize more savings over having a life, then all you'll end up with in the end is lots of money. Wouldn't you rather have some money and some life?

• •

HELP YOURSELF STICK WITH IT

Figuring out what works to keep you motivated is key to being a successful saver. If you've been telling yourself that it's not worth saving unless you have $100 or $500 a month to put away, time to get rid of that nonsense tape. Can you save a dollar a day? Yah, I know the bank won't take your dollar, but at the end of three months you'll have enough to get started with a regular program. Carpool, share a newspaper, skip that coffee, make your lunch at home, and take the money you would have spent and put it in your Savings Jar. When it adds up to $100, it's time to put it to work in an investment of some kind (more on this later).

Get involved with people who are also saving. Whether you join a blogging community like mine at www.gailvazoxlade.com or get together with like-minded people to talk about money and how to achieve your goals, a support system can be key to keeping you motivated.

Set a goal for yourself and then plot your progress. Maybe you'll decide to save $83 a month, so you'll have $1,000 in one year. Get yourself a notebook and make that your Savings Log. Or make a poster—like those posters charities use to track contributions—on which you can highlight your successes. Each time you find an extra dollar or six to put towards your monthly goal, write it in your Savings Log or chart it on your poster.

 ## GAIL'S TIPS: MONEY SET-POINT

Do you have a money set-point? Is there a magical number that triggers you to go spend money? Some people feel safe when they have $1,000 in the bank. For others, the number has to be much higher. But whatever that number is, when you have that much money, you feel it's okay to go blow some dough.

Knowing your money set-point, regardless of how low or high it may be, is important to understanding the psychological triggers that may be stopping you from saving more.

Some people create different accounts for different purposes: their home maintenance fund, their emergency savings, their travel account. One reason they do this is to set a goal for each pile of money, and then make it easy to track their progress to this goal. Another reason is that if they put it all in one place, they'd feel "rich" and be tempted to spend the money. They know their money set-points and have taken steps to work around this psychological marker.

So what's your money set-point? And what are you going to do to get around it?

DON'T TAKE OUT A LOAN

Regardless of how committed you are to saving for retirement, the reality is you've got competing priorities, some of which are shrieking more loudly than others. You've got rent or a mortgage to pay, student loans to repay, and fun to have. Daycare is expensive, you're determined to get that mortgage paid down, and you've been promising yourself a vacation and this is the year. You simply don't have the money to come up with an RRSP contribution. Hey, it happens. Whatever you do, don't fall into the trap of borrowing.

Borrowing to contribute to an RRSP only makes sense if

1. you're in the highest tax bracket AND
2. you can pay off the loan within one year WHILE
3. making monthly contributions to your current year's RRSP.

All three things have to be there. Otherwise, borrowing to contribute to an RRSP is NOT A GOOD IDEA!

I have heard loads of stories from unhappy people who were convinced to borrow to contribute to their RRSPs only to watch the refunds they were "promised" and the payback schedule they thought they would have evaporate. Salespeople and storytellers like to use the highest possible marginal tax rate when figuring out RRSP tax savings. But if you're not in that tax bracket, that's not what YOU will get. And if you're making a large contribution, you might actually get even less on a portion of that contribution if the money you deduct moves you into a lower tax bracket.

You have to ask yourself why a loan is the answer to "not saving." Hey, if you can't afford to take money from your cash flow to put into an RRSP, why can you afford to take money from your cash flow to repay an RRSP loan that also has an interest cost?

Ah, yes, the interest cost. Whenever you borrow money there's a cost. The problem is that salespeople use the tax savings you'll get to minimize the cost of the loan, at least in the minds of people easily lead. If your loan costs you 3%, that's 3% more you have to earn on your RRSP investment just to break even. And since most RRSP loans are variable-rate loans, you could be looking at sharply higher interest costs down the road as rates go up.

Not making a contribution this year isn't the worst thing in the world. You don't lose your contribution room so you can catch up next year or over the next two years depending on how serious you are and how much your cash flow can stand.

Don't be swayed by the hype sold by lenders about the growth you'll miss out on in your RRSP if you skip even a $1,000 contribution you could have made to your RRSP. Just make the contribution as soon as you can out of your own cash flow and everything will be fine. Most lenders' examples assume you never make the contribution so they can use "compounding" to scare you into what you're missing. Don't buy their crap.

As for all those contributions you've never made, it may be tempting to take a big, fat loan to catch up all at once, but you'd be buying a pig in a poke.

When Beverly's bank found out that Bev hadn't been maximizing her RRSP contribution room, they offered her $65,000 to catch up all at once. They showed her a scenario where she would get a $26,650 tax refund that she could use to pay off her outstanding credit cards and lines of credit. It sounded like a really good idea to Beverly. And when they showed her how much she'd have in 23 years when she was ready to retire, she was sold.

Bev's loan would be at 6%. She would make payments of about $720 a month for 10 years to get this loan paid off. But, hey, her money would be inside her RRSP growing on a tax-deferred basis. Beverly was happy in her ignorance because she never bothered to ask a really important question: What's this loan going to cost me?

Browse around on the Internet and look at the loan calculators that many banks offer and you'll find they're happy to tell you what your payment amount will be, but less forthcoming on what the loan will cost when the interest you will pay is added up. You put in how much you want to borrow, for how long, and at what interest rate, and they spit out a monthly payment amount. Hey, that's all you need to know, right? Well, that's what lenders want you to focus on. From their perspective, all you have to figure out is whether you can afford the payment or not. And if you can work that payment into your cash flow, the decision is a no-brainer.

If Beverly took the time to figure out what the loan was actually going to cost her, she'd probably choke. You see, that loan is going to cost Bev about $21,000 in interest. That's a good chunk of what she saved on her taxes by making that

RRSP contribution. BAM, the tax savings benefit of the RRSP has just been significantly reduced.

That assumes that interest rates don't move during the 10 years it takes Bev to pay off the loan. Since the interest rate on RRSP catch-up loans are not set, as rates move up the cost of the loan will increase. If her rate ended up averaging 7%, the loan would cost her almost $26,000 in interest. If her rate ended up averaging 8%, the loan would cost her almost $30,000 in interest. Keep in mind, too, that if interest rates go up Beverly will find her monthly payments going up, putting more pressure on her cash flow.

The other problem with this is that Beverly's income isn't actually high enough for her to get full use of the RRSP tax deduction at the top marginal tax rate the lender used to project her tax refund. As the big fat deduction is applied and her income falls into lower and lower tax brackets, she gets less and less back in tax.

With loan repayments eating up a large slice of her budget pie, will Beverly be able to afford to make her regular RRSP contributions going forward? If the answer is "no," at the end of the catch-up loan she would have to catch up the contributions she didn't make for 10 years while she was repaying the loan. Sounds like a Catch-22 to me.

In a similar boat as Bev? Want to know what you should do?

1. Calculate the amount you would have made in loan payments for your catch-up loan.
2. Use that amount to make contributions to catch up on your unused RRSP room. It may take a little longer to catch up,

but you'll have no interest costs. All your money will be working for you, instead of making a bank more profitable. And you'll be able to invest slowly using dollar-cost averaging to even out your entry costs.

Can you tell that I'm not a fan of catch-up loans? I think they play in to people's needs for immediate gratification. And that immediate gratification comes with a hefty price tag. Saving and investing are long-term, slow-and-steady propositions. If you want to catch up on your RRSP unused contribution room, trim back on your expenses or make enough extra money to sock away what you want. Don't borrow it.

BUILD A BUDGET

I've watched so many people blunder through their lives, spending money without thinking about it and then crying about what they can't have. If you're operating without a plan—read "budget"—you're at the whim of whatever you're dealing with at the moment. Without a plan, it's pretty tough to stay focused on the big picture. Sure you're burnt out and would love a vacation, or you've been studying your nuts off and would love a night out with friends. But if you're spending next week's rent money, grocery money, or telephone bill money to do it, you're going to be very sorry.

Having a budget means you're making a conscious decision about how you really want to spend your money. It's about being aware of how much you have and prioritizing thoughtfully so you can cover the things that are important to you. It isn't about "doing without." It's about "living within" your means.

Making a budget is a bit like doing a puzzle . . . you have all the pieces, and you just have to get them all in the right place. But making a budget doesn't always mean getting it right on the first go. Sometimes you have to move those pieces around to make it work.

The first place to start is by assessing how you've been spending your money. You can do it one of two ways:

1. Track your spending for a month or three.
2. Review your spending for the past six months. This is my preferred method since six months' worth of info is far more revealing.

Once you've got some numbers to work with, you'll plop 'em into the budget, set them against your average monthly income, and then set to work making it balance.

Your budget is broken down into two parts: fixed expenses and variable expenses.

Fixed expenses are the things you pay regularly for which you must cough up a specific amount of money. For example, rent is a fixed expense. So is your car payment.

Variable expenses are the things that change somewhat each month. For example, while you may budget $600 a month for food for your family, that amount isn't fixed since it may fluctuate depending, for example, on the season or what you must buy this month. (Gee, why does all the laundry stuff run out at the same time?)

But budgets can also be broken down along the lines of needs and wants or Must-Haves and Nice-to-Haves. Within your fixed expenses, for example, you may be living in a place that costs you a bundle every month. That's not a need. You need to keep a roof over your head, but you don't need to live in a McMansion. If you can't afford it—if your cost of accommodation is pushing your budget out of whack and there's no where else to cut back—it may be time to call the movers!

Are you ready to make a budget? There's a budget worksheet on pages 132 to 134, or you can go online and use my Interactive Budget Worksheet. Here we go.

1. Take your budget worksheet and enter in your net income (page 19) . . . all of it.

2. Now enter in your fixed expenses, starting with the Must-Haves (use black ink to enter these numbers so they are easily identifiable as Must-Haves):
   • rent or mortgage payment and property taxes
   • car payment
   • insurance

3. Now enter in your variable expenses, starting with the Must-Haves (again, use black ink to enter these numbers so they are easily identifiable as Must-Haves):
   • groceries
   • transportation
   • medical
   • retirement savings
   • debt repayment
   • emergency savings

GAIL'S TIPS

Remember, the Must-Haves are the things that won't go away, so you must plan to have them covered every month. Long-term savings, debt repayment, and emergency savings will change in quantity depending on where you are in your life but they are MUST-HAVES. While you may be tempted to ignore savings if your budget is tight, don't. If you aren't saving a penny now, even a small amount like $25 a month gets you on the right path. Totally ignoring your retirement savings until "things get better" means you're stuck in Not-Saving Land. Just a little is all it takes to cross the border.

You already know how much you're saving for retirement since you figured out your personal savings rate and wrote it down on page 28. And you know how much more you should be saving because you calculated your "gap" in real dollars and wrote it down on page 71. Now we come to where the rubber meets the road. What are you going to write on your budget in the retirement savings line? Will it be what you're comfortable with, what you're already saving? Will you close the gap completely by adding in the amount by which you need to increase your savings? Or will it be somewhere in the middle? And if it is, what's your plan for closing that gap? And by when?

This book isn't about making a theoretical commitment to saving. Maybe. Tomorrow. The fact that you've come this far means you've recognized that you must save. In fact, you've either heaved a huge sigh of relief because you're saving enough, or you're dead down-and-determined to save more. Don't wuss out now. Taking control of your retirement and your future is important. And it's the responsible thing to do. So do it.

4. Go back to your fixed expenses. Time to enter in the Nice-to-Haves (use another colour to enter these numbers so they are easily identifiable as Nice-to-Haves):
   • telephone
   • cable

The Nice-to-Haves are the expenses that you can make go away, although variable Nice-to-Haves are easier to cut back on in the low-income months. But even fixed Nice-to-Haves can be moderated (use your cellphone less, cut down on your cable package for a couple of months) if need be.

5. Go back to your variable expenses. Enter in the Nice-to-Haves (again, use a colour other than black to enter these numbers so they are easily identifiable as Nice-to-Haves):
   • clothes
   • gym membership
   • travel

6. Add up all your expenses.

• •

Sometimes there's a crossover between Must-Haves and Nice-to-Haves, like when your only pair of winter boots are no longer serviceable: then that "clothing" item becomes a Must-Have. This is particularly true if you have kids who will insist on growing. In this case, you put in a Must-Have number to cover the basic needs, and then upgrade it to a Nice-to-Have number for all the extra things you will want. If you have to cut back later on, the Nice-to-Haves have got to go!

• •

7. Subtract your total expenses from your total income.

8. Do you balance? If you're over, you have to either cut back on your expenses or find a way to make more money.

9. To cut back on expenses, start with your Nice-to-Have variable expenses. Trim back. If you're in debt or you don't have the money to save for retirement, you can't afford booze, cigarettes, chips, coffee, lunches out. You will have a very limited entertainment budget, and you'll have to pay for all your fun (sports included) out of that money. Do you balance now? If so, congrats! You've got your template. If not, keep going.

GAIL'S TIPS

If you're working with a variable income, it is at this point that you need to make some big decisions. In your dry months—lowest-income months—you may only be able to afford the basics. In your flush months—highest-income months—you need to

- catch up in some categories of your budget you may have been squeezing, like home maintenance, vacation, clothes, gifts, etc.
- set aside some money to make sure you have an extra pool of cash available for the dry months so you can meet your most basic needs.

The mistake most people make with a variable income is spending every penny when they have a flush month or three. Having lived on less during dry months, they see the flush months as the opportunity to spend, spend, spend. Big mistake. You must first ensure you have the money to see you through the next dry spell. Then you can go shopping!

10. Next, move to your Nice-to-Have fixed expenses. Cut your cable. Cut your phone bill. Get a pay-as-you-go cell plan, or swap texting in and talking out. Do you balance now?

11. Now look at your Must-Have variable expenses: Where can you trim there? Food will come under the knife here. While you still need to feed your family healthy food, if you have not been meal planning and shopping the sales with coupons, you're going to start now.

12. And finally, if you still can't balance, you'll have to find ways to trim your Must-Have fixed expenses or make more money. For example, if your housing costs are high but you really love where you live, could you take in a roomie to help with the costs? Cut your utilities by becoming a power and heat vigilante. Consolidate your car and home insurance, raise your deductible and cut your insurance premiums.

If you can't balance your budget no matter how far back you cut then you simply do not make enough money. Time to get a second job, a third job, or a better job. You have to do WHATEVER IT TAKES. Not making enough and using credit to fill the gap is financial suicide. Not saving anything for the future is an emergency waiting to happen.

 GAIL'S TIPS

. . . .

Some people like to give themselves a "cash allowance" that they can spend any way they want, but that's a license to shop unconsciously. If you're spending the money, you should be thinking about it. You had to work hard for it and no unconscious spending is acceptable, particularly when you're in debt or have no savings for the future.

• •

There are some categories people cut back on so the budget will balance, knowing full well that they'll have to spend the money even if it's not in the budget! They create a budget they know won't work because they don't believe any budget will work. So they leave out categories like clothing, home maintenance, fun, family gifts, medical expenses, and car repairs. And then they blame "the budget" when things don't work.

It makes much more sense to make a plan and stick to it than to make a plan you know won't work. Yes, you may need to adapt on the fly if your "car repair" money hasn't built up enough to cover the cost of the new tires you had to buy. But it's unlikely you'll have to buy new tires, repair the roof, buy the kids new shoes, and cover a birthday all in the same month . . . so as long as you have money accumulating in those pots, you can move it around to make your budget work.

The bottom line is that you can't spend more money than you make. If you can't get the budget to balance, either cut costs or make more money. Debt has to be repaid. And you have to save something both for emergencies and for the long term.

Don't get caught in the mindset that says if you aren't saving a hunky chunk then there's no point. Start small. Anything you put away today is money—plus some return—that you'll have tomorrow. And if tomorrow is a long way off for you, you've got loads of time to make small grains into a heap.

SQUEEZE EVERY PENNY

Very often people have a hard time trimming back their spending because they just love their small indulgences. They don't
realize that even a little less itch-scratching can make a huge
difference given time and the Magic of Compounding. Yah, it's
a motivation thing. So what if I told you that if you're 20 years
old and can find a way to save just $20 a week, you would end
up with more than $150,000. Just 20 bucks.

I bet if you put your mind to it, you can find $20 a week to
put into a retirement savings plan. Come on, tell the truth.
Accumulate it for a month, and voilá, you've got an $80 RRSP
contribution to make. Start at age 25, and by the time you're
ready to quit working 40 years later, that spare change will
have turned into over $100,000!

Finding $20 a week isn't so tough. And it can make a huge
difference to your future.

Let's see how much you could have by giving up something
small and sticking $20 a week or $80 a month (earning 5%)
into an RRSP:

Age	Amount Saved	# of Years	Amount You'd Have
50	$14,400	15	$21,383
45	$19,200	20	$32,883
40	$24,000	25	$47,641
35	$28,800	30	$66,581
30	$33,600	35	$90,887
25	$38,400	40	$122,082
20	$43,200	45	$162,115

So if you started at 35, your $28,800 would more than double. If you started at 30, your $33,600 would almost triple. And at 20 or 25, with between 40 and 45 years to compound, your $20 a week would be worth lots 'n' lotsa money.

SAVE STRATEGICALLY

You've heard me say this dozens of times: Look in the most obvious places for savings and become conscious about how you're spending your money. But there are some other strategies you can incorporate into your savings plan to really come out on top.

People are always telling me they can't find money for savings. Really? Not even $1 a week? I don't believe you. I think if you put your mind to it, if you really, really want to save, you can. Here are some tips:

1. **Get started.** I don't care if you use an envelope, a coffee can, or an old jam jar. Pick an amount and stick it in your container every single week. Whether it's $2 or $10, the trick is to do it religiously, never count it, and don't spend it. EVER. Under no circumstances. You may have to hide it from everyone else so they aren't tempted to dip into your stash of cash.

2. **Live on your pre-raise income.** If you get a cost-of-living increase or a performance raise, pretend you didn't and save the extra money you're bringing home each pay.

3. **Tax your spending.** Like to hit the fast-food outlets or drive-through windows? Keep a container in your car

and every time you pick up a coffee, grab a burger, or hoe through a muffin, drop a buck in your bag. This will be your Fast Food Tax. Hey, if you can find the money for the coffee, you can find the money to save too!

4. **Reallocate your debt-repayment money.** Just paid off a big bill like your car payment or credit card? Assuming you're out of the hole, add half the bill amount back into your budget and save the other half. You're already used to living without that money, so save some.

5. **Save your "savings."** This is one of the things that drives me crazy! People tell me how much they SAVED on sales, using coupons, or just by being a smart shopper and then I say, "So where are those savings?" They look at me with a dazed expression. They laugh and shake their heads. Hey, it's nothing to laugh about. If you just saved $6 at the grocery store by being a savvy shopper, take that $6 and stick it in your SAVINGS container at home. If you don't, you'll just spend it somewhere else and then you won't have saved a penny.

6. **Reward yourself.** If you have the discipline to use a credit card and pay off your balance every month, use a card that gives you cash back or a useful reward. My credit card earns me grocery money. And I just cashed in points from another reward program for coupons for the drugstore and a grocery store. That's over $600 I can stick into my savings.

7. **Use a change jar.** For every transaction you do in cash, you'll get about 50 cents back in coins. Since most people make about 15 to 20 transactions a week, that adds up to about $7.50 to $10 a week. Take your change and put it in your "savings" jar. I know lots of people who use a change jar to save for a holiday. Now, I don't consider this savings since you're going to spend the money. But if it's money you're not going to carry as a balance on your credit card, I'm all for it. If you don't have an emergency fund, this is a great way to get one started. It's also a great way to build up an RRSP contribution. And if you supercharge your change jar by dropping in a fiver at the end of every week, you won't believe how fast that money grows.

8. **Swap a bad habit for a good one.** Love candy? Can't walk by the coffee shop without dropping $3 for a caffeine boost? Smoke, drink pop or booze, or chew gum? Start giving up your bad habit slowly, and reward yourself with a good one as you do. Go from smoking 20 cigs a day to 15, and drop the $2 you didn't send up in smoke into your Good Habit jar. There, you've started to save for the future. Walk past the coffee shop just once and you can add another $3 to your Good Habit jar. Make your lunch at home instead of buying lunch at work and save $4 a day. Hey, that's $20 a week!

9. **Cut your communications bill.** Here is one area where people routinely overspend: telephone, cellphone, cable,

Internet. Cut your bill by $10 a month and now you have enough to start a savings plan. Cut it by $30 and you're three-times smarter.

10. **Save your extra paycheque.** Most people set up their budgets to accommodate two or four paycheques a month, depending on their pay schedule. Sometimes you get an extra cheque in the month. Save it. Sometimes your take-home pay goes up at the end of the year because your payroll deductions go down. Save it.

11. **Eliminate waste.** Most people have things they're spending money on that when push comes to shove they can cut. How much are you spending on that gym membership you aren't using? What about that magazine or newspaper subscription that you keep buying even though you haven't read the stuff that's already piled up? And that auto-renewing website membership?

12. **Buy just a little less often.** Get your hair done once every eight weeks instead of every four to six and you're in the money. Ditto your mani-, pedi-, waxing, tweezing, or whatever other measure you take to make yourself gorgeous. Squeeze all the toothpaste out of the tube. Put a little water in the bottom of the laundry soap bottle and get an extra wash. And each time you do something to save, put that savings in a jar where it can accumulate and you can see how your efforts are paying off.

If you're living close to the bone—you don't have even an extra quarter left over at the end of the day—then you'll have to decide if saving for the future is important enough for you to do whatever it takes to Make More Money! At the end of the day, the only way to have extra money is to trim your expenses or to make more money. And that's a choice only you can make.

BECOME CONSCIOUS OF YOUR SPENDING

Once you're committed to squeezing every penny you can from your budget for saving, you'll be amazed at where you find money. Most people spend without even thinking about it. When I suggest you can find the money you need to save, it isn't a matter of cutting back to the point where you're having no fun at all. But wouldn't it be interesting to see just where the money goes when you're really paying attention? If I told you that by cutting just $5 a day from your spending and putting that money away for an RRSP contribution, you'd have an extra $1,800 a year for investing, would you be interested?

Make yourself up a tracking sheet to see just where your money is going. Put the days of the week across the top and some typical categories down the left-hand side. Include stuff like coffee, snacks, lunch, cigs, gas, magazines/newspapers—everything you spend money on in a typical day. Leave lots of blanks on the left because you'll be amazed at what you'll add each time you whip out your wallet to buy something.

As you go through your week, write down what you're spending. You're going to add it up, so there should be a column on the far right for Total Spent for the week for each category you've included on your worksheet.

Are you surprised at what you're spending? I'll bet you a chocolate truffle you are. And I'll bet you another that you can trim $5 a day out of your spending, no problem.

So is nickel-and-diming it really worth it? Yup. If you save $5 a day, 20 days a month, and put the money in your retirement plan earning just 7%, in 20 years you will have $55,000. Double your savings and you'd have over $100,000.

MAINTAIN BALANCE

All of that said, making a commitment to saving and becoming conscious about spending are part of finding the balance in your financial life. You've heard the saying, "Don't put all your eggs in one basket." If you prioritize any one aspect of your financial life over everything else, you won't have any balance. Typically, young people want to focus on home ownership above all else. If you do, if you don't save for retirement, you don't have enough insurance, or you don't have an emergency fund, it is only a matter of time before your plan falls apart. Ditto if you're in your mid-40s or early 50s and you're hell-bent on getting rid of your mortgage, so much so that you aren't socking any money away for the future. A sound financial plan has a firm foundation that covers all the bases. Putting all your eggs in one basket is a good way to see your plan scrambled if you stumble. (This applies just as much to your whole financial life as it does to your investment portfolio.)

Did you read the book or see the movie about Dr. Doolittle? There was an animal called the pushmi-pullyu (pronounced "push-me-pull-you") with two heads facing in opposite directions. Clearly this creature had difficulty trying to decide in which direction to go.

People face the same kind of dilemma when they're trying to decide whether to pay down their debt or save. And when the media focus on debt repayment heats up, the push to save seems to take a back seat. It shouldn't.

I'm a big fan of finding a balanced approach to handling your money. Doing any one thing to the detriment of another won't create the kind of balance you need to keep you safe. Having some savings is important. And planning for the future is important. Just as important as paying down your debt. I know that lots of people promote the idea that focusing on your debt repayment should be your first priority. I agree that debt repayment should be a top focus. But it shouldn't pull all the light off having a plan for the future.

Skipping years of investment growth on your retirement savings because you're singly focused on debt repayment can mean a huge dollar difference when it comes time to pick up the gold watch. And not having any long-term plan can play serious havoc with your peace of mind. Since I'm a big believer in both compounding return and peace of mind, striking a balance is my default position.

The other thing I believe in is the law of inertia: The law of inertia says that a body at rest will remain at rest until some force acts upon it. And a body in motion will remain in motion . . . well, you get my drift.

As long as you're not saving for retirement, I believe you'll be able to come up with 1,000 reasons not to save: You have to get your student loans paid off; there's a wedding; there's a home down payment; there are kids. The only way to get to a Savings Place is to start saving today. You cannot save $10,000 until you save $1,000. You cannot save $1,000 until you save $100. You cannot save $100 until you save $10.

As for whether it ever makes sense to take the money out of an RRSP to pay down debt? The answer is NO, NO, NO, NO, NO, NO, NO. The tax implications of deregistering the RRSP are too frightening to even think about. I know people who have taken money out of their RRSPs, and they are never prepared for the amount of tax they will have to pay on those withdrawals.

So what if you're out of work and paying no tax at all? If you have no money to make ends meet, making an RRSP withdrawal may make sense for you. Keep in mind that once you take the money out, you can't just put it back in. An RRSP isn't like a TFSA: You don't get replacement privileges.

Of course, if you have unregistered investments—mutual funds, GICs, and the like, that are not in an RRSP—and expensive consumer debt, then it makes sense to sell those investments and pay off the debt. Then rebuild your investments. Take the money you would have used monthly for debt repayment and start an automatic investment plan.

BALANCE RETIREMENT SAVINGS WITH OTHER PRIORITIES

Where did you get the picture of what your life should be? Where did you come up with the ideas you hold as truths about what you should have, should look like, should do?

I meet a lot of people who have expectations that are completely unrealistic, and it makes me wonder where they got their life pictures. Why would a woman who has just graduated from university and hasn't even got a good job yet think it's okay to have a baby, buy a house, and throw herself a big wedding? Why would a young couple believe that the beautiful house they bought (that they could barely afford) isn't good enough and buy a bigger one? And when did the kind of car we drive, the clothes or shoes we wear, or the neighbourhood we live in become such a reflection on us that we're willing to pretend things are fine when we're not setting aside a penny for retirement?

With all the stuff just waiting to be bought, the question becomes this: Are you really willing to spend whatever it takes to have it all right now, regardless of the impact on your financial health and your future?

It may take revamping the picture you have of your life. If you have painted a picture for yourself that you simply cannot afford, it's time to paint a new picture—one that you can feel good about.

It's lovely to think that a beautiful home, a late-model car, a cottage, boat, and basement full of entertainment equipment is ours for the having, but the reality is that for many people our grasp exceeds our reach. I can't afford that car that parks itself and I know it. To go out and lease one would mean I'd have to scrimp in other areas—most likely on my savings and my emergency fund—and I'm not prepared to do that.

Ditto an annual vacation. While it's a lovely idea, and it may be hard to watch others head south while I'm stuck shovelling snow, the reality is that putting it on credit isn't an option for me. So I've painted myself a picture that includes a family vacation somewhere every few years, depending on how I'm doing financially. I save up the money and come back with no regrets.

 GAIL'S TIPS

• •

While it's fine to use your money for any purpose you wish—it's your money, you get to decide what to do with it—it's important not to sacrifice your long-term goals for your short-term desires. If you're saving for a home, instead of putting your whole RRSP contribution into your "home ownership RRSP" this year, divide it equally between home ownership and retirement. Yes, it will take a little longer to get into your dream home. But when you do, you won't be behind the eight ball in terms of retirement planning. Striking the right balance in saving is just as important as in life. A little into each pot will serve you well.

• •

So, what pictures did you paint that are getting you into trouble? What did you imagine your life would be like, only to wake up to some hard realities that have you scratching your head? And how do you feel about having to change your expectations? If you aren't willing to revamp your picture, how are you planning to make it work?

Perhaps the hardest part of taking control of your retirement and your future is the first step: honesty. You must honestly look at the picture you've built and the impact it's having on your financial stability. If you're balanced and in a good place, then the picture's a keeper. If you haven't been able to figure out how to come up with even $20, $35, or $50 a month for the future, it's time to get out a fresh canvas and start painting a new picture.

Sure, finding the money to save for the future means you can't spend it now on something you think you want. But having money in the future gives you options, so not saving is a really bad idea.

RRSP OR MORTGAGE PAYDOWN?

Sometimes balance means using more than one strategy to achieve what you want. While you may be hell-bent on paying off your mortgage, if you do so and have no money to save for retirement, you're missing the mark. Did you know that over 50% of Canadians with a mortgage don't contribute to an RRSP? It seems that once that mortgage note is signed, getting rid of what can be the single largest debt we ever take on becomes of paramount importance. But building a retirement nest egg is just as important as getting rid of that mortgage. It all comes down to time. The longer you have your mortgage, the more interest you'll pay. And the earlier you begin saving for retirement, the more money you'll accumulate.

The answer to the question of whether to contribute to your RRSP or pay down a mortgage does not have to be either/or. While the math shows a considerable interest savings by applying money to your mortgage principal, the growth of an RRSP contribution is also impressive. So here's a sensible compromise.

Why not make the maximum RRSP contribution you can

afford from your cash flow and then use the proceeds from your tax refund or the savings in taxes you achieved by filling out a Form T1213 to pay down your mortgage? It's a little like having your cake and eating it too. You can

- save for retirement and secure your future,
- earn tax-sheltered income,
- reduce the amount of current income tax paid, and
- reduce the amount of interest to be paid on the mortgage, as well as the amortization term, by applying the tax refunds received to pay down the mortgage.

Let's say you decide to contribute $5,000 a year to your RRSP, so you make monthly contributions of $417. And let's say your marginal tax rate is 30%, so you'll receive a tax refund of $1,500 each year. Slap that refund against your $200,000 mortgage on which you're paying 8%.

Assuming an average return of 6% each year on your RRSP portfolio, in 25 years your $125,000 in contributions will have grown to about $289,000.

By applying your $1,500 refund to your mortgage, you'll save over $60,000 in interest and have your mortgage-burning party five years sooner.

It makes a lot more sense to work towards both objectives than to grapple with the issue of which should be a priority. You can save for retirement, minimize your current tax bite, and earn tax-sheltered income. You can also have your home paid off faster and save scads of interest on your mortgage. See, you *can* have your cake and eat it too.

SLOW AND STEADY

Sometimes when people decide to stop wasting money, they find that they can cut back for a while, living life by the book, scrimping and saving. Inevitably, they end up blowing their brains out on a shopping spree, vacation, or some other unplanned spending that they just HAD to do to deal with the deprivation they were experiencing. It's the Yo-Yo Effect. Spend nothing, nothing, nothing, and then . . . BAM! . . . too much.

Part of the problem is the fact that people perceive they can fix their financial problems by cutting back to the bone and having no fun while they ratchet up their savings. When they hit some "magic" amount they feel is appropriate, the relief and sense of accomplishment are the signals to go and blow their brains out. What a waste of energy!

People, it isn't about going with*out*, it's about living with*in* . . . your means, that is. Nobody says you can never buy a cup of coffee again. Or a new pair of shoes. Or a nifty new cellphone. Well, I don't, anyway. (I know there are some rabid Don't-Spend-a-Cent maniacs out there, but I'm not one of them.) To live a balanced life you do have to come to terms with how much you make, how much you want to save, and how much you have to spend on your needs and then your wants.

If you want to take a fabulous vacation with your family, then you should. You absotively, posolutely should. Let's say you want to go away for two weeks. You've budgeted the trip: airfare, lodging, food, transportation, insurance, and whatever else, and you've found you'll need $3,200 to pull it off. How much do you have in your existing budget that you can put towards your trip? If you can afford to save $137.50 a month, it'll take you about 24 months to come up with the money to pay for the trip in full.

And for each $137.50 you manage to save somewhere else, you'll eliminate one month of waiting.

You could, just for one month, trim back your groceries by $100 and put that in your Vacation Savings Account. You could decide to turn down your thermostat, drive less often, or make your next set of gifts, and slide your savings into your Vacation Savings Account. Now you're not depriving yourself of anything . . . you're accumulating money to make a dream come true and when it does, the vacation will be the reward. And you're doing it in small increments so you don't end up sacrificing the long-term savings you need to ensure your future is just as rosy as your present.

Putting aside money for a vacation, for paying down debt, for having a life, it's all the same thing. It's about finding the money from your existing cash flow to achieve a particular goal. Make the steps manageable . . . like finding $137.50 . . . and you won't be overwhelmed.

 GAIL'S TIPS

Can't afford a vacation away from home? You can still have loads of fun while you save tons of money if you opt for a staycation. That's when you stay home and pretend you're on vacation. Imagine you're in a foreign city and drum up the same excitement as you would if you were seeing local things in a place you had to pay thousands of dollars to get to. Pick a start and end date for your staycation to make it official. Declare a choratorium—no one has to make their bed, do the dishes, or vacuum. (Consider hiring a cleaning service for midweek to whip the house back into shape.) And pack your schedule full of fun and fabulous things to do.

Communities everywhere have productions ranging from high school musicals to community theatre to professional theatre. Plan to take in a night at the theatre, or go to the symphony, the opera, or a rock concert. With all the money you're not spending on accommodations, you can have a ball.

• •

When you make the commitment to save for your retirement, it shouldn't be about having no life now because you're living in fear that you won't be able to eat when you're 82. It should be about having SOME of the things you want now, and some of the thing you'll need in the future . . . like food. It's about accepting that the future won't take care of itself. It's about balance.

Of course, you also have the option of finding a way to make more money to put towards your goals. Whether it's taking a part-time job on weekends or doing something from home so you don't have to be away from the kids, there are lots of ways to bring in an extra $137.50 a month. Choose something that you like to do anyway—ref a hockey game, get into the party-planning business, write on a freelance basis, sew, weed, or become a part-time companion to a shut-in—and you can make more and have fun.

Once you've busted your butt to find the money to save, you'll then have to decide how to put that money to work for you so that it grows. This can be a huge stumbling block since the choices are numerous and the information confusing. I'm going to make it easy-peasy for you in the next chapter.

Budget Worksheet

Monthly Income $

Net salary #1   _____

Net salary #2   _____

Self-employment income   _____

Investment income (dividends/interest)   _____

Rental income   _____

Spousal support/child support   _____

Government benefits (GST, child allowance, etc.)   _____

Pension income   _____

Other   _____

Total Monthly Income   _____

Expenses

Rent/mortgage payment   _____

Property tax/water/sewage   _____

Gas   _____

Electricity   _____

Other utilities   _____

Home insurance   _____

Home maintenance and condo fees   _____

Other home expenses   _____

Car payment #1   _____

Car payment #2   _____

Other vehicle payment(s)   _____

Auto insurance   _____

Other vehicle insurance   _____

Vehicle maintenance and licence   _____

Expenses (*cont'd*) $

Parking   _____

Gas   _____

Transit costs   _____

Taxis/trains/tolls/tickets, etc.   _____

Telephone/long distance   _____

Cellphone(s)   _____

Cable/satellite   _____

Internet   _____

Child care   _____

Tuition   _____

Pet care (grooming, vet, food, insurance) _____

Spousal/child support   _____

Kids' activities   _____

Allowances   _____

Life insurance   _____

Disability insurance   _____

Health insurance   _____

Other insurance   _____

Medical/dental/prescriptions   _____

Long-term savings   _____

Emergency savings   _____

RESP savings   _____

Total debt repayment (excl. cars and mortgages) _____

Charitable giving   _____

Bank fees   _____

Food   _____

Personal care   _____

Personal grooming   _____

Expenses (*cont'd*) $

Restaurants _____

Sports & Hobbies _____

Interests & Clubs _____

Clothing _____

Entertainment _____

Gifts _____

Travel _____

Total Monthly Expenses _____

Monthly Income _____

− **Monthly Expenses** _____

= **Monthly Surplus or Deficit** _____

8

NARROW DOWN YOUR INVESTMENT OPTIONS

Saving even the smallest amounts of money consistently will eventually result in a nice heap of savings. Mix the Magic of Compounding with time and discipline and you can achieve wonders. You may not notice the exact moment when your automatic monthly deposits transfer into a worthy sum, but it will happen. The first step is to get yourself a bucket (an automatic savings plan) and start using it to move your sand from one pile to another, so that at the end of the day you've got a heap.

You've figured out how much you should be saving, and you've gone through your budget with a fine-tooth comb to find the money to save. The next steps are to understand the different types of investments available and figure out what suits you. With a good understanding of what's available and what's really important to you, it won't be as hard as you might have imagined to take the next step: buying the investments that will help to make your retirement savings grow.

So let's look first at the investment options available.

KNOW WHAT'S AVAILABLE

Have you ever bought an investment? Some people are very experienced with the world of investing, some not so much. Knowing what you know and figuring out what you need to know are big parts of being a smart investor. If you think you've never been an "investor" you may be wrong.

Do you have a savings account? That's an investment. Anything that puts your money to work to earn more money is an investment. Just because it has no risk attached and the returns are paltry doesn't mean it isn't an investment. It's just a very low-risk, low-return investment. If you've bought a GIC, you're an investor. And if you've bought a Canada Savings Bond, you're an investor. Again, these are pretty low-risk, low-return investments, but they put your money to work to earn more money, so they qualify.

There are loads of investments from which to choose when it comes to putting your savings to work. So many, in fact, that you may feel completely overwhelmed by the choices. Take heart. Once you know a little more about yourself, including your risk tolerance and your time horizon, you can narrow down the options and choose the ones that will work best for YOU. We'll get to that, but first let's look at some of the options.

Savings Accounts: Low Risk, Low Return, Very Liquid

The traditional savings account will give you access to your money when you need it, but will pay you only a small amount of interest, and only if you're smart about it.

This is where you'll keep money you may need to access at any time and for any purpose. It may be where you keep your home maintenance money. It's the account you use to save for an emergency. It can be a run-of-the-mill Big Bank savings account, but only if you're a total dope and don't mind earning next to nothing on your money. It can be a high-interest account that pays more interest, most often offered by non-traditional banks like ING Direct, PC Financial, or Ally. Or it can be a TFSA, using a savings account option. And if you've parked your RRSP deposit in a "savings" option while you figure out what to do with it next, you're in a traditional savings account, even if it has "RRSP" stamped on it.

GICs: Low Risk, Slightly Higher Return, Medium to Low Liquidity

Next up the line in terms of most people's investment experience is the Guaranteed Investment Certificate (GIC) or Term Deposit (TD). Term Deposits usually run from 30 days to 364 days. When you get into talking "years," you're also talking GICs, which typically run from one to five years. You'll earn a little more interest by locking up your money, but you won't have access to that money at the drop of a pin. And if interest rates go up during the time you have that money locked up on deposit, you won't get the higher rate . . . not until it comes time to renew. So you're taking a chance—assuming what's called "interest rate risk"—but you're willing to do so because your hard-earned moolah is completely and utterly safe, assuming you're covered by deposit insurance.

Once you get past the deposit products, like savings accounts and GICs, the field opens up.

 GAIL'S TIPS

• •

"Liquidity" is the ability to get at your money quickly. A savings account is very liquid because you can walk on over to the ATM and pull some money out. An investment like a GIC that ties up your money for five years is far less liquid unless it has a "redeemable" feature that let's you break the term you've chosen.

• •

Fixed Income Investments: Medium Risk, Potentially Higher Return than GICs, Medium to Low Liquidity

When you buy a stock, you have no idea exactly how much you'll make. But when you buy a bond or a mortgage as an investment, you know exactly what your return will be: It's the interest rate quoted. If you buy a bond paying 3%, that's what you'll get, assuming the bond is of good quality and doesn't default. Investments that state their return right off the top are called "fixed income" investments because your return is guaranteed if you hold the investment to maturity.

GAIL'S TIPS

Savings accounts and redeemable GICs also fall into the category of fixed income investments. However, because they are very liquid and the principal is guaranteed, they can be converted to cash quickly, so they are referred to as "cash" or "cash equivalent." Having some money in "cash equivalent" investments means you can respond to emergencies or can take advantage of buying opportunities because you have cash on hand without having to sell other investments. Every investment portfolio should have some money in cash equivalent options, just in case. It's kind of like having an emergency fund for your investment portfolio.

Growth: Medium to High Risk, Potentially Much Higher Return, Medium to High Liquidity

You can buy investments like stocks, which fall into the "growth" category because they offer you a bigger opportunity to "grow" your money by offering the potential for higher returns. There are many flavours of "growth," from "blue-chip" stocks, which offer you slow and steady growth, to "high-fliers," which offer the appeal of a very high return very quickly. But growth investments also come with a significant risk: the potential to lose some or all of the money you invested. Depending on the quality of the stock you buy, you could watch your money grow steadily, or suffer the yo-yo of speculation.

GAIL'S TIPS

• •

While the liquidity on stocks is very high—you can buy and sell them quickly—the price at which you'll buy or sell can also be quite volatile. That's why, despite their high liquidity, growth investments should be thought of as "long-term" investments.

• •

Mutual Funds: Low to High Risk, Low to High Return, Low to High Liquidity

Wow, that description doesn't tell you very much does it? That's because the way a particular mutual fund behaves depends on the investments held within the fund portfolio. If you buy a mutual fund that invests in Treasury bills and commercial paper, it'll act like a savings account. If you buy one that holds bonds or mortgages (or both), it'll act like a fixed income investment. If you buy a mutual fund that holds shares of companies, it's going to behave like a growth investment, reacting to whatever the underlying shares do.

The Index: Medium to High Risk, Potential for Medium to High Return, High Liquidity

There are a variety of indices that measure how the stock market is doing. And there are a number of index-based investments that have been created to mirror these indices. When you buy "the index" using something like an ETF (electronically traded fund), you're buying how the whole index is doing as opposed to trying to pick a particular group of stocks. It's kind of like buying a mutual fund, but without the fund manager or the high fees.

 GAIL'S TIPS

• •

There are as many investment options available as there are colours of flowers and flavours of food. It can be mighty confusing for some folks. And the investment marketplace can be a pretty risky spot if you don't know what you're doing. Sticking with what you know, and learning about what you think you want to do next before you act, makes much more sense than jumping in with both feet only to find out later that you made a mistake. If you don't understand an investment well enough to explain it to a 15-year-old, you shouldn't be buying it.

• •

Each investment option or vehicle is just a different way to put your money to work. And each has positives and negatives. Some are in favour some of the time and out of favour at others. Some have more risk attached but offer the lure of substantially higher returns if you have the stones to handle the risk. If you're an investor, it's all about finding ways to put your money to work so it earns you more money. If you're a smart investor, it's also about understanding your unique needs, including your risk tolerance and investment time horizon. And this is exactly what you're going to learn in this chapter.

WHAT INVESTING ISN'T

Here's what investing is not. Investing is not gambling. When a gambler lays his money on the table, he's betting on an outcome that is uncertain. He might win. He might lose.

Hang on a second. That sounds an awful lot like investing in some stocks. What about those penny stocks? Those high-risk ventures? There's no way to know what the outcome will be.

And this is exactly the problem with how some people invest. If you buy based on a hot tip, you're not an investor, you're a gambler. If you buy based on what everyone else is doing, you're not an investor, you're a gambler. And if you haven't done your homework, you're not an investor, you're a gambler.

True investing isn't an easy thing to do. It takes research, analysis, and hard work. You only put your money down once you're pretty sure (no, you're not guessing or hoping or wishing) that there's a reasonable expectation of profit. The risk isn't completely gone, but you've done enough digging to know exactly what those risks are and what to watch for so you'll know when it's time to sell your investment. Or you'll have a smart body doing this for you.

Everybody wants to make money. The stock market, the bond market, the commercial paper market all look like easy ways to take a dollar and turn it into ten. There's no sweat, no calluses, no aching back. It seems to happen by magic. And everyone has a great story of easy money made in an up market.

⏰ GAIL'S TIPS

· ·

If you find you want to broaden your investment horizons, you may want to find a body who can help to
guide you through the wide range of choices you have
(see Chapter 9). Regardless of whether you're a do-
it-yourselfer or you're counting on the expertise of an
advisor, you must keep learning so you become more
comfortable with investing.

I know it can feel pretty risky handing your money
over to some Joe. That's why you have to do your
research and find a body you can trust. And that's why
you'll keep learning about investing: so you can know
when you're being fed a line of crap.

· ·

Investing may look easy, and it can be if you know what you
want and know the rules. But it can also be incredibly complex. After all, if winning the stock market game was a no-
brainer, all the guys who are trying to convince you to become
an active trader would have their own islands somewhere
because they'd be rich! They could just make it big and spend
the rest of their lives in Margaritaville, right?

Investing, particularly when you're talking about investing
in the stock market, takes hard work, research, and discipline.
It takes real smarts. Not every idiot can make money in the
markets. And it takes a knack, which is why guys like Warren
Buffet become stars.

For most of us, the investment world is big and scary. But letting fear get the better of us and staying away from opportunity can be a mistake too.

The answer to the investment dilemma is to

- figure out your time horizon,
- know yourself, and
- clarify your objectives.

FIGURE OUT YOUR TIME HORIZON

Your time horizon is the length of time during which you will not need to touch the money you are investing. An emergency fund has a short-term time horizon since you may need it at a moment's notice. It has to be accessible and it has to be stable.

If you have three years or less until you need to get your mitts on the moolah, you have a short-term investment horizon. If you can keep your hand out of the cookie jar for up to 10 years, you have a medium-term horizon. Longer than 10 years is considered a long-term horizon.

If you're saving for retirement, your time horizon will depend on how long it'll be until you retire. A 25-year-old has a long-term investment horizon. She won't need that money for 40 years or more. But a 60-year-old is likely to need at least some of the money in as little as three or four years. That's a short-term investment horizon.

The longer you have until you will need to use the money, the more time your investment has to even out its return. That's why time horizon is important, particularly when you're investing in equities—think stocks and stock-based mutual funds.

Time horizon isn't fixed. As you get closer to using the money, your time horizon shortens and your investment choices must change. If you don't respond by changing your investment mix, you could be deeply shocked when it comes time to use the money. If the markets have changed direction just when you need to move to cash, you could find yourself liquidating at fire-sale prices.

Time horizon is particularly important when you're talking about investing in anything for which there is no principal guarantee. Time lets you ride out the natural volatility associated with investments whose value tends to rise and fall. Most often these are equity investments, although if you're trading bonds (instead of holding them to maturity), volatility could apply to them too. Since equities have historically outperformed all other types of investments over the long term, people with an investment horizon of more than 10 years can benefit from the potentially higher returns equities offer, because they have the time to ride out the natural volatility associated with the market.

While The Spurts often like to draw a direct co-relation between your age and your time horizons, you shouldn't. It's less about how old you are and more about when you'll need to spend the money. Even if you're 50 years old, depending on when you need to cash out so you can use your money, you may still have a 20-year investment horizon ahead of you. That leaves you the flexibility to choose from both fixed income and growth investments.

Ready to decide on your time horizon? Remember, each time you invest money you have to decide how long it'll be before you'll need to use that money. Since we're talking about retirement savings, you're now going to decide how long it'll be until you actually need to spend the money you're saving.

 GAIL'S TIPS

● ●

Remember, just because you retire does not mean you will immediately need access to all your money. If you retire at age 55, you're likely to live in retirement for another 25 to 30 years. So some of your money will continue to have a long-term investment horizon.

● ●

Identify Your Time Horizon

☐ I have less than five years until I retire and need access to this money. I have a short-term investment horizon.

☐ I have between five and 10 years until I retire and need access to this money. I have a medium-term investment horizon.

☐ I have more than 10 years until I retire and need access to this money. I have a long-term investment horizon.

KNOW YOURSELF

The single biggest mistake you can make when it comes to investing is to not know who you are and stay true to your own needs for safety and return. Everyone measures risk differently since it is relative to our personal circumstances, which is one reason why you have to be brutally honest with yourself and have a big-picture perspective when you're measuring your risk tolerance. While one person may think investing $25,000 in stocks is okay, another may balk. If $25,000 represents your total savings, or if it represents a substantial part of your annual disposable income, you will be more likely to experience a sense of risk. On the other hand, if that $25,000 represents only 10% of your overall investment portfolio, capital risk is far less of a problem and volatility may not be an issue at all. So, when a financial loss would be deeply felt, the level of risk is much higher.

It's been my experience that people with a low risk tolerance in the physical sense are also likely to have a lower risk tolerance in the financial sense. People who will jump off tall towers with large elastic bands tied to their feet seem to be those who are equally willing to leap into roller-coaster stocks. So that can be your first clue.

Just because you're willing to throw caution to the wind doesn't mean you should. Some people take risks because they don't understand that they are taking risks. Or perhaps it is because they face extreme risk over and over that they develop a higher tolerance—almost numbness—to risk. The opposite is also true. People who are very afraid think they are taking more risk than they actually are. So daredevils may have to pull back a little to create a more balanced investment strategy while scaredy-cats may have to force themselves to venture a little further out on the limb.

If we allow risk to simply be an emotional issue, we are left to the vagaries of our emotional spectrum without any weight given to the role that our intellect, experience, and wisdom can play in helping us better understand why we take the risks we do. The intelligent application of a sound risk profile can keep said emotional body on the straight and narrow when it comes to investing. After all, knowing who we are means we can counter the fear and reel in the greed when they start to get the better of us. We can work through the regret scenarios and lay a path while we're still on this side of sane. We can start smart and stay smart.

Gail Rant! I dislike the Know Your Client form most financial institutions use to supposedly help clients identify their risk tolerance. Short and superficial, those risk profiles quickly and without much thought identify investors as high, medium, or low risk. But these questions aren't intended to help you determine how you actually feel about investing and the risks you're willing to assume. They are cover-your-butt pieces of paper designed to protect institutions from reprimand when a client's portfolio goes south and he gets ticked. The Know Your Client form isn't enough to create a clear profile of who you are as an investor. To be able to stay the course with an investment plan, you must not only dig deeper, you must have confidence in the risk-profiling exercise.

Want to get an idea of what your risk profile looks like? Take the following test.

Gail Warning! This risk assessment contains language you should be familiar with as an investor. If you are not familiar with specific terms such as "diversification" or "capital," it means you are currently a relatively inexperienced investor. For any question that has language you do not understand, you should automatically choose "a" as your answer.

1. I know my overall income will increase in the future.
   a) No way
   b) Maybe not
   c) Maybe
   d) Probably
   e) Definitely

2. I like the idea of a guaranteed return and stability.
   a) Definitely
   b) Probably
   c) Maybe
   d) Maybe not
   e) No way

3. Investing in the stock market is like gambling. There's no way you can win.
   a) Definitely
   b) Probably
   c) Maybe
   d) Maybe not
   e) No way

4. I want investments that are on the leading edge: high tech, pharmaceuticals, emerging countries.
a) No way
b) Maybe not
c) Maybe
d) Probably
e) Definitely

5. In choosing an investment for my son's or daughter's post-secondary education fund, I'd stick with
a) GICs
b) government bonds and insured mortgage-backed securities
c) corporate bonds
d) stocks or equity mutual funds
e) speculative investments

6. I think the professional money management and added diversification provided by mutual funds make them a smarter investment than individual stocks.
a) Definitely
b) Probably
c) Maybe
d) Maybe not
e) No way

7. I have too much debt.
a) Definitely
b) Probably
c) Maybe

d) Maybe not

e) No way

8. I'm happy to settle for less return if I know my capital is completely safe.

a) Definitely

b) Probably

c) Maybe

d) Maybe not

e) No way

9. I have

a) four or more dependants

b) three dependants

c) two dependants

d) one dependant

e) no dependants

10. I plan to retire in about

a) 0 years—I'm currently retired

b) 1 to 5 years

c) 5 to 9 years

d) 10 to 19 years

e) 20 years or more

11. My net worth is

a) under $15,000

b) $15,001–$50,000

c) $50,001–$150,000

d) $150,001–$350,000

e) more than $350,000

12. My emergency fund is equal to

a) 1 to 2 months' salary or less

b) 3 to 6 months' salary

c) 7 to 9 months' salary

d) 10 months' to one year's salary

e) more than one year's salary

Score Your Test

Score one point for every "a" answer, two for every "b," three for every "c," four for every "d," and five for every "e."

If you scored:

- **More than 45: Very High-Risk Investor.** You likely have both the inclination and the money to take on more risk. You could look at aggressive-growth stocks, start-up companies, commodities, options, and investment real estate. But don't go overboard on the risk side. You'll still need to allocate at least a portion of your portfolio to lower-risk investments or your high risk tolerance could put you at high risk to lose it all.

- **Between 41 and 45: Moderately High-Risk Investor.** You can stomach a pretty high level of risk. Combined with enough time and income to cover your losses, you can afford to incorporate investment equities to create an aggressive portfolio.

- **Between 36 and 40: Average-Risk Investor.** While you have some tolerance for risk, you like to keep control over your investments too. Create a mix of long-term investments that have a history of strong and steady performance. Blue-chip stocks, high-grade corporate bonds, and mutual funds with low levels of volatility will all appeal to your investment personality.

- **Between 31 and 35: Low-Risk Investor.** You don't much fancy risk. Maybe you're getting closer to retirement. Maybe you've suffered some familial instability. Or maybe your income has fluctuated somewhat in the recent past. To be comfortable, you must stick with high-quality investments that are pretty secure: a home, high-quality bonds, government-backed securities.

- **Less than 31: Very Low-Risk Investor.** You hate the idea of assuming any risk. Stick with certificates of deposit, government bonds, and high-paying savings accounts.

There's no point in putting your money into investments that will keep you awake at night. Only gamblers and ignorant investors do this. Smart investors know they must balance the return they want to achieve with their personal risk tolerance. Some people are more safety-conscious than others. Some people are determined to go for the highest possible returns, damn the risks. You need to understand your own feelings about how much risk you're willing to tolerate—and how much you need to accept—to achieve the returns you desire.

When it comes to analyzing our investment risk tolerance, what we think is true and what is actually true are often different. Here's another test for risk tolerance, which you must think about a little harder. Let's see how closely your results from this test mirror those from the first test. If your results are remarkably different, use this test's results. If there is only a slight difference, think about what's different. If there's no difference, congratulations! You've got a good handle on your investment personality.

Gail Warning! This test also contains quite a bit of sophisticated "investment" language. If you don't understand the question, or any of the options given as answers, you should automatically choose "a" as your answer.

1. Six months after you buy an equity mutual fund, the value of your investment increases by 20%. Your first reaction is to
a) sell it and take your profit.
b) hold it, hoping the price goes up even farther.
c) buy more, since there is real money to be made here.

2. You've bought a stock that's dropped 20% of its value in the past two weeks. You
a) sell it and get into something safer.
b) hold it, hoping the price goes back up.
c) buy more. The lower price is a real deal.

3. You've lost $500 at the track. How much are you willing to risk to get back your $500?

a) $0

b) $250

c) $500

4. You and two friends are each holding one ticket for a lottery. One of those tickets has won $100,000, but you don't know which. You

a) sell your ticket to one of the other guys for $1,000.

b) agree to split the money three ways.

c) go for broke. You want the whole $100,000.

5. You're offered an opportunity to invest in a new diamond mine. If the mine is successful, you could get back 50 to 100 times your investment. If it's a dud, your investment would be worthless. There's a one in five chance that the mine will come in. How much would you invest?

a) Nothing.

b) One month's salary.

c) Six months' salary.

6. You've inherited a house that's a wreck but located in a very good part of town. You

a) sell it.

b) put some money into it and then rent it until you can sell it for a good price.

c) tear it down and finance a new home, then hope it sells for a handsome profit.

Give yourself one point for each "a" answer, three points for each "b" answer, and five points for each "c" answer.

If you scored:

- **More than 23 points.** You'd be considered a high- to moderately high-risk investor and could call yourself "growth-oriented." While you're probably very comfortable with high degrees of risk when there are potentially higher returns, don't get cocky!

- **Between 14 and 23 points.** You'd be considered an average to low-risk investor, so call yourself "balanced." You're willing to take calculated risks but you can't stomach losing too much money. Make sure you balance those risks with some safer investments.

- **Less than 13 points.** You're a very low-risk investor, so call yourself "conservative." You're uncomfortable with risk, so stick with the investments you know well and that guarantee your principal.

Rate Your Risk Tolerance

Okay, time to rate your risk tolerance. In light of the results you got from taking these two tests, which of the following terms are you most comfortable using to describe yourself:

☐ I am a growth-oriented investor.

☐ I am a balanced investor.

☐ I am a conservative investor.

It's human nature to measure risk against the opportunity to win. The bigger the potential downside, the bigger the pot of gold must be to persuade us to take the chance. An individual's sense of risk decreases as the potential for reward increases and odds improve. Yes, odds play a part too. Would you invest $50 to win $5,000,000 if your odds were 100 to 1? What if your odds were 2 to 1? Most people would have no problem investing $50 for a 2 to 1 chance of winning $5,000,000. What would you do?

A lot of people who were tired of low interest rates threw caution to the wind and jumped into the stock market without so much as a glance back at their risk tolerance. They ended up being badly bitten in the last market correction. Since investment returns had been extremely attractive (the opportunity to win was high) and the markets had performed pretty steadily (the odds were in the equity investor's favour), people leapt into the markets with little thought to the downsides. Later, when markets corrected—as all markets do—they fled for their lives, losing money they would never have lost if they had held tight to a long-term strategy, because they missed the subsequent upturn the market took (as it inevitably will).

It's important that you understand how much risk you can stand before you start waking up in the middle of the night with the sweats. That's no way to live. And it's no way to invest.

You should not only know how much risk you're prepared to take, but also understand exactly what you're investing in.

And don't think that because something has been recommended to you, that it's okay to buy it. If you don't understand what you're buying, you shouldn't be buying it. If you don't know the risks involved, you shouldn't be buying it. And if you think it's too good to be true, you shouldn't be buying it.

UNDERSTAND YOUR RATE OF RETURN

While I encourage everyone to stay true to their investment risk tolerance and only choose investments with which they are comfortable, it's important to know the impact even a small increase in return can have on your retirement savings.

Let's say you can come up with $500 a month for your RRSP.

You Invested @		5%	7%	9%	11%
15 years	$90,000	$133,644	$158,481	$189,203	$227,345
20 years	$120,000	$205,517	$260,463	$333,943	$432,819
25 years	$150,000	$297,755	$405,036	$560,561	$788,067
30 years	$180,000	$416,129	$609,985	$915,372	$1,402,260
35 years	$210,000	$568,046	$900,527	$1,470,882	$2,464,148
40 years	$270,000	$763,010	$1,312,407	$2,340,660	$4,300,064
45 years	$300,000	$1,013,219	$1,896,297	$3,702,439	$7,474,207

Look at how much of a difference even 2% more on your portfolio will mean in terms of dollars you'll have to spend when you're done working. Your savings can work hard or harder depending on the types of investments you choose and the returns you generate over the long term.

If the first thing that springs to mind is, "Where the hell am I going to get 11% in this day and age?" my answer is: probably nowhere, unless you're prepared to accept substantial risk. But "this day and age" isn't what you'll be living in for the next 25 or 30 years. The economy will change. Interest rates will go up and down. So will returns on the market. What's important to understand is that the harder your money works in terms of return, the more you'll have. And the "more" can be "substantially more."

Also look at the difference an extra five years of compounding can make at the various rates of return. If you can't stomach the idea of moving into an investment that pays you 9% with its associated risk, that's fine. Just reconcile yourself to working a little longer. You can end up with even more at 7% just by putting more time on your side.

There are lots of ways to skin the cat. You can go for a high return. You can go for a long period of compounding. You can go for higher contributions. Whatever you choose has to work for YOU. But you can accomplish your goals, assuming they are realistic and you work towards them consistently.

CLARIFY YOUR OBJECTIVES

Don't let anyone tell you that because you're young you should be aggressive in your investment style, that you have heaps of time to ride out market ups and downs, and that you're a fool to sit on the sidelines and make do with whatever pathetic interest rates your local bank is offering. That's none of their damn business. Only you can decide what you want to invest in, what you feel comfortable with, and what you're going to do with YOUR money.

Never mind what your cousin Sally is doing. Or how much money your next-door-neighbour Mike made last year in the markets. What do you know about investing? What do you understand about risk and how much are you prepared to take? And how long do you have until you need to use the money.

Time to clarify your objectives and then make some decisions about what you're going to do with your money.

Based on your time horizon and your risk profile, you'll fall into one of nine investment profiles.

If your time-horizon is	And your risk profile is	Turn to pages
Short-term	Conservative	161 to 162
Short-term	Balanced	162 to 163
Short-term	Growth-oriented	163
Medium-term	Conservative	163 to 165
Medium-term	Balanced	165
Medium-term	Growth-oriented	166
Long-term	Conservative	166 to 168
Long-term	Balanced	168 to 170
Long-term	Growth-oriented	170 to 172

Short-Term Horizon with a Conservative Risk Profile

Anyone with a short-term investment horizon needs to stay with investments that allow them to maximize their liquidity. You have to be able to get at your money when you need it. And you can't afford to take chances with that money. You're a preservationist. You want to make sure your money is safe. So you'll be looking at the investments in the first tier of the investment pyramid on page 173.

Within the first tier, some investments may offer slightly higher returns than others depending on where you buy them. One of the most significant differences in these investments is whether or not your principal will be totally guaranteed.

Savings and chequing accounts held at a Canadian financial institution that is a member of the Canada Deposit Insurance Corp. (CDIC) are covered for up to $100,000 if the institution goes bust. As long as you stay under the limit, and you invest with a company that's CDIC insured, your principal is safe.

While bank failures are few and far between in Canada, they are not unheard of. If you want to be dead sure your money is absolutely safe, you want to be covered by CDIC. Foreign banks with branches in Canada may also be members of CDIC, and if they are, you are covered. If not, you're SOL, so check before you put your money on deposit.

GICs and term deposits are covered, too, as long as the term of the deposit is five years or less. The $100,000 limit is for all your non-registered accounts with a single bank. So if you have $80,000 in a savings account and another $80,000 in a chequing account, you are covered for only $100,000—not the $160,000 total.

Joint accounts are covered separately, so if you have $100K in your savings and chequing accounts, and then open up a joint account with your son, partner, or best friend, the joint account is covered for another $100K. Savings accounts and GICs held in an RRSP or TFSA are also covered separately.

All other investments in Tier 1 are reasonably safe, but there's no guarantee. Even money market funds, whose unit values are managed to remain stable, have a teeny-tiny bit of risk attached. Only you can decide if you're prepared to accept that risk for the potential of a slightly higher return.

Short-Term Horizon and a Balanced Risk Profile

You probably wish you could find a way to earn a higher return than you can get on a savings account or redeemable GIC. But you can't. Not if you've got a short-term investment horizon. You've got to stick with the investments in the first tier of the investment pyramid on page 173.

If you want your money available when you need to use it, you've got to stay with investments that have no volatility at all so you don't put your capital—the amount you initially invested—at risk. And you can't lock your money up to get a higher return because you'll just end up tying your own hands behind your back when you need to use the money.

You may not be thrilled with the rate of return you're earning, particularly during periods of very low interest rates. And you may not even be earning enough to stave off inflation, but if you've got a short-term horizon, that's the price you'll pay if you want to be sure your money is there when you need it.

Remember, however, that we're talking about the money

you know you're going to need in the short term. If you have a pool of money, you may not need to use it all at once. So even if you are retiring in a couple of years, it is only the money you'll need to pull to spend, and your emergency fund, that will have a short-term horizon. The rest may have a medium- or even long-term horizon depending on when you're going to use the money.

Short-Term Horizon and a Growth-Oriented Risk Profile

It may drive you crazy to watch your money "languish," earning a pittance in return when you know there are all sorts of other options available, but resist the urge to plunge into the markets. If you have a short-term horizon, the fact that you've got a growth-oriented investment personality doesn't even come into the decision. You've got to stick with the investments in the first tier of the investment pyramid on page 173.

Think about it. If you take a chance on an investment that may generate a higher return, what will you do if the investment tanks or the market is down just when you need to use the money? You'll kick yourself for having taken too much risk with your short-term money. Just take a deep breath, resolve yourself to doing the right thing, and stay true to your time horizon.

Medium-Term Horizon and a Conservative Risk Profile

With a medium-term investment horizon, you've got a little more time to play with, but as a conservative investor you need to choose investments that let you sleep at night. Since you can't stomach taking chances with your money, you aren't willing to assume any capital risk. You'll be looking at the investments in the first and second tiers of the investment pyramid on page 173.

Capital risk is the potential for losing some or all of the original money you invested (which is your "capital.") People with a huge fear of capital risk tend to stick to tried-and-true investments like term deposits or GICs, only to then run smack-dab into interest rate risk.

Interest rate risk is the risk that interest rates will rise and you will be locked in to a lower rate. Another risk is that if you've invested at a high rate, interest rates may be a lot lower when it comes time to renew. The way to minimize this interest rate risk is by laddering your investments.

Trying to decide what GIC term will work out best for you? Trying to catch the highest rate can be tough. Don't chase your tail. Ladder instead.

Laddering means splitting your investments over a variety of terms. If, for example, you have $5,000 to invest, you'd put $1,000 each into a one-, two-, three-, four-, and five-year GIC. This creates what's called a "rolling maturity cycle." Every year you'll have some money coming due that you'll invest in a new five-year GIC.

If interest rates have gone down, only one-fifth of your money is immediately affected. If rates have risen, you have the opportunity to take advantage of those higher rates because you have some money coming due for renewal.

Laddering reduces your exposure to interest rate risk because having a variety of maturities reduces the impact of interest rate fluctuations. It also gives you some liquidity since you'll always have some money maturing each year. Best of all, the approach is very disciplined; you won't be chasing rates.

Medium-Term Horizon and a Balanced Risk Profile

With a medium-term investment horizon and a balanced risk profile, you need to choose investments that will let you get to your money when you need it but offer a higher rate of return. So you'll be looking at the investments in the first, second, and third tiers of the investment pyramid on page 173.

Since you're likely to need your money in 10 years or less, make sure you match the maturity date of your investments with your end-use date.

A bond's maturity refers to the specific date on which your principal will be repaid. Maturities can range from one day to up to 30 years. So maturity ranges are often categorized as short term, medium term, and long term.

You can't "go long" on a bond if you're going to need your money in the medium term. You'll have to stick with maturity dates that match your time horizon.

Sure, you can sell a bond before it matures, but that's like trading a stock: If the market isn't quite right, you could lose money on the sale. When you have a medium-term horizon, assume you're holding the investment to term. If you do get the opportunity to sell for extra profit, you can just clap your hands together in glee. But don't bank on it.

Medium-Term Horizon and a Growth-Oriented Risk Profile

Despite having a growth profile, your medium-term investment horizon means you need to keep the majority of your money in investments that won't be affected by changes in the economy or in the markets. Volatility is your enemy.

When the value of an investment goes up and down a lot over a short or medium amount of time, that investment is said to be volatile. Volatility is the market gyration that most people dread and the one we tend to overreact to. Even investors who say they're prepared to deal with some volatility can have the air sucked right out of their lungs if the market goes into free fall.

You might expect things like speculative stocks to be volatile, but you might be surprised at where else volatility raises its scary head. Industry-specific mutual funds, such as mining or technology funds, or funds that invest in small-capitalization companies can be very volatile. And even bonds can be volatile if interest rates start to jitterbug.

With your growth-orientation, you'll be looking at the investments in the first to fifth tiers of the investment pyramid on page 173. However, because of your medium-term horizon, consider holding no more than 30% of your portfolio in investments above the third tier.

Long-Term Horizon and a Conservative Risk Profile

With a long-term investment horizon and a conservative risk profile you won't need to get to your money for a long time. You can afford to ride out the highs and lows that come with changes in the economy and in investment markets. And you'll be concerned about ensuring that your money doesn't lose its buying power because your return doesn't keep up with inflation. So while your instinct may be to stick your money under your mattress, you need to be brave.

Initially, because you're a conservative investor, you'll want to stick with things in the first two tiers of the investment pyramid on page 173. But don't let your emotions make all the decisions for you. With loads of time, you have the option of taking just a little more risk. You may start with only 5% of your portfolio in a less traditional investment, but start stepping outside your comfort zone. Read about mutual funds and index investing. Choose one or two investments that you are interested in but may be afraid to commit to, and track them. How would you have done if you'd put just 5% of your long-term investment dollars into that option? As you become more familiar with those investments (because you're keeping track of them), are you getting a little more comfortable with the idea of diversifying your portfolio and adding a little more growth?

Wish you had the guts to stomach the equities market so you could earn more on your money? There's a mutual fund product called a segregated mutual fund that offers a principal guarantee on anywhere from 75% to 100% of your principal if you hold your investment for the full term specified, usually 10 years. So if you invested $30,000 in a 10-year seg fund with a 100% guarantee, you would receive your initial investment plus profits made from market gains assuming the market goes up. If the value of the seg fund is below $30,000 when your fund matures, the principal remains protected but your investment would have earned no return, so you are assuming some risk. You can periodically "lock in" the protection on the principal when the policy has escalated in value, and this resets your 10-year guarantee period. You will pay for this guarantee either in the form of a higher management expense ration (MER) or as a separate fee.

Long-Term Horizon and a Balanced Risk Profile

With a long-term investment horizon and a balanced risk profile, you'll be willing to assume risk for the opportunity to earn a higher return. However, you should also balance principal protection by using some lower-risk, fixed income investments. You'll be looking at the investments in the first to fifth tiers of the investment pyramid on page 173. The percentage you hold in each of the different types of investments—or your asset mix—will dictate how much risk you assume and how well your portfolio does in terms of return.

Concentrating your portfolio on one or two types of investments is a great way to lose your shirt. Diversification—or buying a mix of investments—not only brings a higher level of portfolio safety, it minimizes the impact of violent swings in the markets. There are a number of ways to diversify your portfolio:

- By the type of investment. Different investments have different levels of risk associated with them. The more risk you're willing to assume, the higher return you may earn on your portfolio. Low risk often also means low returns.

- By the quality of investment. The higher the quality of your investment, the less likely you are to lose money and the lower your potential return. Quality ranges from very safe ("A++" rating on a bond) to highly speculative (junk bonds).

- By region. You can invest in Canada, North America, Europe, Asia, or other regions of the world. If you're looking for steady growth, sticking with a well-developed economy is more in keeping. If you're willing to speculate, an emerging market may be more to your liking.

- By currency. Having investments denominated in another currency means you can profit (or lose) depending on the strength of the Canadian dollar relative to those other currencies.

- By level of liquidity. Holding some long-term deposits, such as strip bonds or equity mutual funds, along with some shorter-term investments, like Treasury bills, reduces your exposure to risk by giving you access to some money when you may need it. The last thing you want to do is sell in a down market. Having investments that are easy to liquidate without loss is the way to reduce the impact of a volatile market.

How you choose to diversify—how much of one investment type you choose over another, for example—is reflected in your "asset mix."

Your investment portfolio could look like either of the following, or anything in between, and it'd be right if it were right for YOU:

- 10% cash, 60% fixed income (Tiers 1 to 4), 30% growth (Tiers 5 and 6)

- 10% cash, 45% fixed income (Tiers 1 to 4), 45% growth (Tiers 5 and 6)

A long-term horizon also means you can "go long" or invest in longer-term maturities (15, 20, or 30 years) on bonds.

Long-Term Horizon and a Growth-Oriented Risk Profile

As an investor, the world is your oyster. You can use any investment on the pyramid (page 173) as long as you can explain how it works. A lack of knowledge is your only barrier. Never buy anything you don't understand well enough to explain to someone else.

Diversification is key to ensuring your portfolio performs well. Diversification refers to putting your money in different types of investments with returns that aren't affected by the same thing. If one of your investments goes south, the odds are good that at least one other will have turned a nice profit.

Like investors with a long-term horizon and a balanced risk profile, you can diversify your portfolio in several ways:

- By the type of investment. Different investments have different levels of risk associated with them. The more risk you're willing to assume, the higher return you may earn on your portfolio. Low risk often also means low returns.

- By the quality of investment. The higher the quality of your investment, the less likely you are to lose money and the lower your potential return. Quality ranges from very safe ("A++" rating on a bond) to highly speculative (junk bonds).

- By region. You can invest in Canada, North America, Europe, Asia, or other regions of the world. If you're looking for steady growth, sticking with a well-developed economy is more in keeping. If you're willing to speculate, an emerging market may be more to your liking.

- By currency. Having investments denominated in another currency means you can profit (or lose) depending on the strength of the Canadian dollar relative to those other currencies.

Within the world of growth investments, you'll still have to modify your choices based on just how much risk you're prepared to take. You can have a slow-and-steady growth portfolio made up of blue-chip stocks from well-established companies, or you can have a very aggressive (even speculative) portfolio full of penny stocks and junk bonds. Only you can decide what will work for you.

Good sense demands that you not put all your money at risk by jumping into speculation too quickly, but as long as you've done your homework and you're prepared for what you may lose, hey, it's your money. Just don't blame the market if your hard-earned dollars evaporate. The market didn't do you in. Your aggressive approach to investing did.

How you choose to blend the investments in your portfolio is called your "asset mix" or "asset allocation." There is no straight-up rule for how to mix your assets, since every investor is different. And whole books have been written on the subject. The most important thing to understand is that how you mix your assets has to be dictated by what you want your investments to do.

A slow-and-steady investment portfolio might hold 10% in cash, 30% in investments from the first four tiers of the investment pyramid, and 60% in investments from Tier 5.

A high-growth portfolio might hold 10% in cash, 20% in Tiers 1 to 4, 40% in Tier 5, and 30% in Tiers 6 and 7.

An extremely aggressive growth portfolio might hold 10% in cash, 25% in Tiers 1 to 4, 25% in Tier 5, and 40% in Tiers 6 and 7.

While newspapers and websites are full of the latest hot investments with their through-the-stratosphere returns, these are anomalies. You're far better off choosing an asset mix that will work for you than chasing after individual investments that make you look like a genius. You need to have realistic expectations so that you don't end up taking more risk than you can actually tolerate.

THE INVESTMENT PYRAMID

TIER 7
Futures,
precious metals/
gems, emerging
markets, speculative
stocks, speculative corporate
bonds, collectibles, small-cap
stocks, undeveloped land, puts
and calls

TIER 6
Region-specific mutual funds,
industry-specific mutual funds or sector funds

TIER 5
Quality growth mutual funds, income property, large-cap
stocks, royalty trusts, index-based investments such as
ETFs or index funds

TIER 4
Balanced funds, high-grade preferred shares, high-grade convertible
securities, corporate bonds rated "A" or higher, segregated funds

TIER 3
Triple-"A" rated corporate bonds, mortgages, mortgage funds, fixed income funds

TIER 2
One- to five-year GICs, strip bonds, bond funds, bankers' acceptances, government bonds

TIER 1
Savings accounts, term deposits, redeemable GICs, Canada Savings Bonds, money market funds, Treasury bills

Gail Warning! What you don't know can hurt you. If you are not familiar enough with an investment to be able to explain it to someone else, you should not be buying that investment. Buying something you don't understand is dumb, Dumb, DUMB! Don't do it.

If you're not happy with the returns you're generating, because you feel they are too low to achieve your goals, spread your wings by doing the following:

1. Learning more about the investments in the next tier up.
2. Moving on up slowly once you feel comfortable with those investments.

 GAIL'S TIPS

• •

You may need to take a little rest at this point. You've done a lot of thinking and your brain is probably tired. This investing stuff can be quite the climb if you've never done it before, or if your range has been very limited. Go for a walk. Give yourself some time to breath. When you come back I'll still be here and you'll be ready to make some big decisions. Off you go . . .

• •

DECIDE

Now that you know your time horizon and your risk profile, it's time to choose an investment or a group of investments that are going to do some work for you.

If you don't know Jack and you're a chicken to boot, stick with the tried and true interest investments like GICs. That doesn't mean you just walk into a bank and plunk down your money, taking whatever they offer. Do your homework and check out what a bunch of different companies are offering. Then show some chutzpah and negotiate for a good rate. If my kid can do it, you can do it.

One December, my then 15-year-old daughter, Alex, got notice of the auto-renewal of her GIC. The interest rate the bank had renewed at was a pathetic 1.5%. I coached her on what to say when she went in to negotiate a better rate.

"I'd like you to cancel this GIC and credit the money to my savings account," parroting me with all the confidence she could muster. "If you're only going to give me 1.5%, I'll move the money somewhere I can earn more."

The CIBC rep was respectful and brought up her file. "If you want to go for a longer term, I can offer you a better rate."

Alex looked at me with huge question marks in her eyes. I stayed quiet. The rep continued, "If you'll lock in for two years, I can offer you 4.25%." I nodded slightly and smiled.

"I'll take it," said Alex.

Subsequently, interest rates continued to fall and Alex continued to gloat over the fact that she was earning about 3% more than was currently being offered. All she had to do was show some gumption and ask for what she wanted. You can too.

Asking for what you want is an important part of being a smart consumer, and the fact that you're consuming "investments" means you should be prepared to push the envelope to get what you want. And that includes an education. It's your advisor's responsibility to ensure you know what you're buying, so make sure you ask as many questions as it takes to feel comfortable.

🔔 GAIL'S TIPS

• •

Based on a bunch of studies that have been done on just how knowledgeable investors are, most investors don't have the experience, training, or time to be able to select investments and know when to buy and sell those investments to make a profit. Enter mutual funds as a solution. Since mutual funds are professionally managed, you don't have to be concerned with the day-to-day decisions required to ensure your portfolio performs well. Knowledgeable managers with years of experience do the tough work of investment analysis and market watching. With in-house analysts and research staff to review financial and economic data, managers are able to sift into the securities that represent the best value.

That assumes, of course, that your knowledgeable professional actually knows what the hell they're doing. Based on the performance of some funds, one has to scratch one's head. What DID they do with all that money they were supposed to be spending on research? And today's star can turn into tomorrow's dog pretty quickly.

If you're not convinced that active management is the way to go, or you're loathe to pay the fees, then buying an index may be the best decision for you.

• •

If you decide that mutual fund investing is right for you, you can buy a mutual fund at just about any financial institution. But don't just give 'em your money, cross your fingers, and hope. Read the prospectus and ask lots of questions. And before you buy a mutual fund. . .

1. check the fees you'll pay. Mutual funds can have a number of fees attached. From front-end commissions to deferred sales charges, these fees will eat into how much you end up investing. You should ask for a list of all the fees associated with a mutual fund before you plunk down your money.

2. know that past performance is not a guarantee of future performance. But what a manager's accomplished in the past can give you an insight if you know what to look for. And what you should look for is the fund's year-over-year returns.

There are some mutual funds that perform in the top quartile over and over. So a good look at a fund's long-term track record is far more useful than any of those top-performer rankings from last year. Don't buy the nonsense about average returns. If you were to put one hand on a block of dry ice and the other on your stove, a mutual fund salesperson might say that on average you are comfortable. Hmm. Average rates of return obscure long periods of both underperformance and overperformance relative to the long-term trend. What you want to look at is the year-over-year performance of the fund you're interested in buying.

	2010	2009	2008	2007	2006	2005	2004	2003	2002
Fund A	10.0%	7.8%	8.6%	5.4%	-3.1%	11.5%	12.0%	9.9%	5.4%
Fund B	23.1%	9.4%	-12.7%	22.3%	21.3%	-24.8%	16.1%	25.2%	-12.7%

Average Fund A: 7.55%

Average Fund B: 7.46%

Fund A has a much more consistent performance year-over-year than does Fund B. While Fund A never returns more than 12%, when you average its returns for the nine years, it comes out to 7.55%. Fund B has several amazing years of earning over a 20% return, but it has some real stinkers, and averages out to almost the same.

If you were to look at these two funds' average returns, you might be convinced they're virtually identical. Nothing could be further from the truth. Fund A has a consistent performance. Fund B's manager may produce some great returns in a few years, but the overall performance of the fund is erratic. And each of those stellar losses is wearing away the amount you have invested.

Buying a mutual fund that's going to do well over the long haul doesn't have to be an exercise in dart-throwing. Do a little research. Take a good look at how the funds you're considering have performed over the medium or long term compared with their peers. And make sure you're looking at each year's return, not just at averages. If you understand how mutual funds work, and what the mutual fund you're buying is trying to accomplish, you're much more likely to pick a fund that you can stick with. And investment wisdom says that a buy-and-hold strategy is the most sensible alternative. Another says that investing smaller amounts over time makes more sense than dumping a bunch of money into the markets all at once. And the way to do that is to dollar-cost average.

DOLLAR-COST AVERAGING

Dollar-cost averaging is a complex name for a simple investment technique. Rather than accumulating a large sum of money before making an investment, you invest small amounts at regular intervals.

Let's say the unit value of a mutual fund fluctuated like this over a 12-month period:

Month	Unit Value ($)
January	12.00
February	13.20
March	13.40
April	9.50
May	9.40
June	8.60
July	9.70
August	10.25
September	9.35
October	10.50
November	12.20
December	13.00

If you saved $80 a month and invested $960 in this fund in December, you would be paying $13 per unit and could therefore buy 73.8 units. But if you invested $80 a month, here's how your acquisitions would look:

Month	Unit Value ($)	Units Purchased
January	12.00	6.66
February	13.20	6.06
March	13.40	5.97
April	9.50	8.42
May	9.40	8.51
June	8.60	9.30
July	9.70	8.24
August	10.25	7.80
September	9.35	8.55
October	10.50	7.61
November	12.20	6.55
December	13.00	6.15

By dollar-cost averaging, you'd be able to buy 89.96 units for an average price of $10.92. You would have 17 units more than if you made your total purchase in December. At December's unit price, that's a return of $221 on an initial investment of $960. Pretty good, isn't it? The key is this: The average purchase price is less than market average because you buy more units at a lower price.

The big upside to dollar-cost averaging is that you don't have to worry about investing at the right time. But if you want it to work effectively, you have to use it as a long-term strategy and stick with it! Don't let market performance shake your trust. It's a great system.

BUYING YOUR INVESTMENTS

While GICs and mutual funds are sold just about everywhere, segregated funds are sold only through insurance companies. And if you decide to buy the index or invest directly in stocks and bonds, you'll either need a broker or a discount brokerage account.

If you're pretty wary about investing in anything but the tried and true, know that as your knowledge about investing grows so too may your tolerance for risk. It's a natural evolution. The more you understand how various investments work, the less fear you feel. It isn't a foregone conclusion, mind you, and you should always stay true to your risk tolerance. But if you've worked to learn more about investing and you feel ready to take on more risk for the opportunity to earn more return, then you'll want to start looking at things like balanced mutual funds or perhaps creating your own mix using the index and direct investment in bonds.

Okay, you know what you want to buy and you know doing so steadily over time is a better idea than saving up the money and plumping it all down at once if you intend to buy mutual funds. You also know that you have to ask lots of questions and expect clear explanations if you want to grow your knowledge so you can grow your money.

Now that you know, all that's left is to do.

9

EXECUTE YOUR PLAN

When I was young, I was a great procrastinator. There was lots of time, and I knew everything would get done eventually. There was no great rush, no sense of time running out. Why do today what you could put off until tomorrow?

I'm not going to categorize all young people as procrastinators. But when you're young, you do have a distorted sense of the time available, which makes it easy to let things slide. And with competing priorities, it can be hard to focus on something like retirement, which seems so far off.

Stop thinking about it as retirement planning. Think of it as saving. If you've been procrastinating about getting started because you think you can't save enough to really matter, get over it. Anything you save now is better than not saving at all. And you have to get started to put momentum on your side. Research shows that having higher income doesn't mean you're any more likely to save. Saving isn't just about money. It's about attitude. And without the commitment to having something in the future, the amount of income you earn has very little to do with long-term savings success.

If you've been holding off because you're confused about what to do or how to do it, well, that's why you're reading this book, right? You've learned why starting early is so important, and you've decided on which mix of investments will work best for you. But there are still some things you need to learn about, like whether an RRSP or a TFSA will work best for you. To know that you have to understand how your tax rate affects your decision, so read on.

UNDERSTAND YOUR TAX RATE

We have a graduated tax system in Canada, which means that the more you earn the more tax you pay. Everyone wants to pay less tax but not everyone is prepared to try to understand how our tax system works. For the most part, I believe in leaving this area to the specialists because it is sooo complicated it makes even my eyes glaze over. But you need to understand, at the very least, how taxes are calculated, so you don't get taken in by marketing ploys designed to convince you to beat the Tax Man by making your local bank rich.

Marginal Tax Rate

Your Marginal Tax Rate is the rate of tax you pay on the last dollar you earned. For 2009, the Federal (not including Provincial) tax rates were

- 15% on the first $40,726 of taxable income +
- 22% on the next $40,726 of taxable income (on your taxable income between $40,726 and $81,452) +
- 26% on the next $44,812 of taxable income (on your taxable income between $81,452 and $126,264) +
- 29% of taxable income over $126,264

As your income increases, you pay a higher rate of tax on each level of income. The more you make, the more tax you pay. And since the income you earn from investments held outside a registered plan is added to your income from all other sources, every additional dollar of investment income is taxed at the HIGHEST rate applicable to your total income.

Provinces Charge Tax Too

Each province also has its own tax system. For example, if you live in British Columbia, you'll pay an additional

- 5.06% on the first $35,716 of taxable income +
- 7.7% on the next $35,717 +
- 10.5% on the next $10,581 +
- 12.29% on the next $17,574 +
- 14.7% on the amount over $99,588

If you live in Ontario, the tiers look like this:

- 6.05% on the first $36,848 of taxable income +
- 9.15% on the next $36,850 +
- 11.16% on the amount over $73,698

And if you're a resident of New Brunswick, your provincial tax tiers are

- 9.65% on the first $35,707 of taxable income +
- 14.5% on the next $35,708 +
- 16% on the next $44,690 +
- 17% on the amount over $116,105

Of course, your provincial and federal rates are combined. If you live in Ontario, it means your tax tiers looked like this for 2009:

- 21.05% on the first $36,848 of taxable income +
- 24.15% on income between $36,848 and $40,726 +
- 31.15% on income between $40,726 and $64,882 +
- 32.98% on income between $64,882 and $73,698 +
- 35.39% on income between $73,698 and $76,440 +
- 39.41% on income between $76,440 and $81,452 +
- 43.41% on income between $81,452 and $126,264 +
- 46.41% on income over $126,264

What It Means to YOU

Okay, what does all this mean?

Well, if you lived in Ontario and made an RRSP contribution of $5,000, and you were in the lowest tax bracket, you'd get a tax deduction of about $1,052.50.

$$5,000 \times 21.05 = 105,250$$
$$105,250 \div 100 = 1,052.50$$

But if you were in the bracket where you paid 35.39% tax, you'd get a deduction of about $1,769.50.

$$5,000 \times 35.39 = 176,950$$
$$176,950 \div 100 = 1,769.50$$

Beware Bad Examples

Sadly, whenever RRSP calculations are done, the examples often use the highest marginal tax rate to demonstrate how big a bang for your buck you can get. But that doesn't hold true if you're in a lower tax bracket, or if most of your income is in a lower tax bracket so your average tax rate is lower.

 GAIL'S TIPS

• •

Your average tax rate is calculated by dividing the total amount of income taxes you paid by your total income. The average tax rate incorporates taxes paid at all levels of income, so naturally it will be less than the marginal rate.

• •

I've worked with people who have been "promised" higher tax refunds simply because the person demonstrating the tax savings didn't ask for or verify the client's marginal tax rate, or how much of their income would be taxed at the highest rate, and chose instead to use the highest rate to make the biggest impression.

One couple I know was advised to take out an RRSP loan, the majority of which they would then pay off with their tax refund. However, because the tax rate used in their example was higher than their actual tax rate, they didn't get back as much money as they thought they would, and ended up being stuck with RRSP loan payments they simply couldn't afford.

THE IMPACT OF YOUR TAX RATE

Since every deduction you claim reduces your marginal tax rate, claiming a big fat deduction in one year may mean that some of that money may not work as hard. If claiming even a part of a deduction moves you to a lower marginal tax rate, the remaining amount to be deducted will be calculated at that lower rate. We'll just look at the federal rate to make this as simple as possible.

Remember, the federal rates are as follows:

- 15% on the first $40,726 of taxable income +
- 22% on the portion of taxable income between $40,726 and $81,452 +
- 26% on the portion of taxable income between $81,452 and $126,264 +
- 29% on the portion of taxable income over $126,264

Okay, let's say you made $45,000 and wanted to claim an RRSP deduction of $7,000. Since the income you earn over $40,726 is taxed at 22%, the first part of your deduction ($45,000 – $40,726 = $4,274) would be calculated like this:

$$4,274 \times 22 = 94,028$$
$$94,028 \div 100 = 940.28$$

The rest of your deduction ($7,000 – $4,274 = $2,726) would be calculated at the lower rate, like this:

$$2,726 \times 15 = 40,890$$
$$40,890 \div 100 = 408.90$$

So you'd get a deduction of ($940.28 + $408.90 =) $1,349.18.

But if you'd just done the simple calculation using your highest marginal tax rate for the whole deduction, you would have believed with all your wallet that you'd be getting back ($7,000 × 22% =) $1,540 and you'd be very disappointed. You'd also have less to pay off that loan you were convinced to take out because of all the money it would save you in taxes.

If you're planning to take out one of those whopping catch-up loans because you've been convinced it's the best thing since sliced bread, please, please do the math on the deductions correctly so you aren't left holding a bag of debt when your refund comes and it's less than you thought it would be.

GAIL'S TIPS

• •

It may be exciting to fill out your tax return and find that the Tax Man owes you a whopper of a refund. Makes you want to do a happy dance, right? But if you're getting a refund, it means you PAID TOO MUCH TAX. You gave the government an interest-free loan.

Time to get to know Form T1213. This form requests permission from the Tax Man to have your employer reduce the amount of income tax taken off your paycheque every month. If you can demonstrate that you're eligible for certain recurring deductions that will reduce your tax bill at the end of the year, you can trade in your tax refund for more take-home pay. So if you're making monthly RRSP contributions by way of pre-authorized withdrawal, you're eligible.

You'll have to fill out the form and send it to the Tax Man each year. The best time to send in the form is in October or November for the following year. Once you're approved, the Tax Man will provide instructions by letter to you, which you then give to your employer, who will adjust your pay for the remainder of the year.

Getting a tax refund may feel good, but when you think that the government has been using your money without paying a red cent in interest, you'll realize that taking control is way more satisfying. Get the form, fill it out, and keep your money!

• •

RRSP VS. TFSA

Once upon a time, the RRSP was the only game in town when it came to saving for retirement. Then in 2009, the Tax-Free Savings Account (TFSA) was born. Within six months, Canadians had opened up 3.6 million TFSAs and had stockpiled over $12 billion in savings. Wow! Talk about a good idea catching on fast!

Ever since, thousands of trees have fallen to the debate over which is better. Here's where you get to decide which is better for YOU. But first you have to understand how these two plans operate so you can make an informed decision. Yes, I said "plans," not "investments."

I swear I'm going to smack the next person who tells me they invested in an RRSP. After all these years of explaining what an RRSP is, how it works, and why you should have one, people still don't get it.

It isn't really the public's fault. It's the fault of the media and of financial institutions, which continue to encourage people to "invest" in RRSPs. Well you can't. RRSPs don't have a return. The underlying investments you will buy do.

Okay, here I go, one more time. I'm going to simplify this as much as I can.

Imagine you have a box and a red umbrella.

Now imagine that you take a $20 bill out of your wallet and stick it in the box. That's what you do when you put your money in a savings account. Now slide the box under the opened umbrella. That's what you do when you put your money in an RRSP. The savings account is the investment. The RRSP is the plan registration.

Instead of a box, you could just as easily have put your money in a shoe (a term deposit) or a plastic bag (a mutual fund) or an envelope (a stock or bond). The investment is where you put the money to work.

The RRSP is the red umbrella that lets you grow that money on a tax-deferred basis.

Now slide the box out from under the RRSP. You've just de-registered that money by taking it out from under the RRSP umbrella, so you're going to owe some tax. The RRSP simply protects both the money you put in and the income you earn from tax, like the umbrella protects you from rain.

The money that goes under the RRSP umbrella isn't taxed in any way. If you have paid tax on that money through your payroll deductions at work, the Tax Man will give you that tax money back, which is why people get a tax refund when they contribute to an RRSP.

If you contribute $2,400 to your RRSP each year and your marginal tax rate is 20%, you'll get a tax break of $480. You can use that $480 to pay down your mortgage, boost your emergency fund, or give a head start to your next RRSP contribution. Or you can put it towards your next vacation.

Since nothing under the umbrella is taxed, the income you earn is tax-deferred too. This is the reason why any money under the RRSP umbrella grows more quickly than it can outside of an RRSP.

Step out from under the umbrella and you'll get wet. Take your money out from under the RRSP registration and you'll pay tax on both what you put in and what you've earned.

A TFSA is an umbrella of a different colour. The money you put under this yellow umbrella isn't tax deferred, so you don't get a tax benefit for making the contribution. But all the income earned under the yellow umbrella is tax-free. You never have to pay tax on it. Never, ever.

What Tax-Deferred Growth Means

The beauty of both an RRSP and a TFSA is in their tax-deferred growth. If you're 40 now and you'll be retiring in 25 years, a $2,400 a year contribution—that's only $200 a month—with an average return of 5% will give you just over $120,000, which is about $16,000 more than if you'd invested outside an RRSP or TFSA.

If you're 35 now and will have 30 years for your RRSP/TFSA to grow, you will have just over $167,000, or $27,000 more.

If you're 30 now and will have 35 years for your RRSP/TFSA to grow, you will have almost $228,000, or $44,000 more.

And if you're only 25 now and your RRSP/TFSA will have 40 years to grow, that $2,400 a year will grow to over $300,000, $67,000 more than if it were not under the umbrella.

Okay, so both an RRSP and a TFSA give you a big bang in terms of compound growth. But how do you decide which is right for you? Read on.

When You Can Contribute

You may contribute to your RRSP at any age, provided you have earned an income, up until December 31 of the year in which you reach age 71. In the case of a Spousal RRSP, you have up to December 31 of the year in which your partner turns 71. The contribution deadline for an RRSP is 60 days from the beginning of the following year. So, for 2011, you have to make your contribution by February 29, 2012. For non-leap years, the contribution deadline is March 1.

You have to be 18 to contribute to a TFSA, and you must make your contribution for the year by December 31 of that year.

 GAIL'S TIPS

• •

While some people think you have to be over 19 to contribute to an RRSP, this is a myth. This misunderstanding came about because people under the age of 19 aren't allowed to make an over-contribution to their RRSPs. However, anyone in Canada who has earned income and has filed a tax return, up to age 71, has RRSP contribution room. That includes kids with a paper route, those that babysit, and children who have promising modelling or television careers. As long as you file a tax return, you're building up RRSP contribution room.

• •

How Much You Can Contribute

There's a formula that applies to RRSP contribution limits. You're allowed to contribute up to 18% of your earned income (this is one time when gross income is important in your calculations) from the previous year up to the annual maximum. For 2010, that annual limit was $22,000.

If you made $30,000 last year, you'd multiply that by 18% to get $5,400, which is the maximum you could contribute to an RRSP this year assuming you didn't have a company pension plan or any unused contributions from previous years. To get all the way to the $22,000 contribution limit, you'd have to earn over $122,000 a year.

There's no formula for calculating how much you can put into a TFSA: Everyone can put in up to $5,000 a year, and limits are going to be indexed to inflation in $500 increments. However, it is up to YOU to keep track of your contributions. The Tax Man will know if you go over the limit and will charge an over-contribution fee payable on your next tax return. So don't go over your limit.

Sometimes people inadvertently go over the allowable RRSP contribution limit, and that's why the $2,000 lifetime over-contribution limit exists. You can deduct the $2,000 over-contribution in future years, but if you exceed the $2,000 over-contribution amount, a penalty tax of 1% per month will be levied on the excess amount.

People over-contribute for all sorts of reasons. It may be because a contribution you made and the amount your employer is contributing to another fund pushed you over the limit. Or you may have joined a company pension plan mid-year and forgotten to stop your individual automatic savings. Or you may simply have miscalculated. Whatever the case, you need to take steps to fix the problem.

You can simply withdraw the offending amount from the RRSP. Your withdrawal will be subject to withholding tax but you'll get that back when you file your next tax return. If you want to avoid the withholding tax, fill out Form T3012A "Tax Deduction Waiver on a Refund of Your Undeducted RRSP Contributions" and mail it to the Tax Man. Once they review and approve it, they'll send it back, and you can take it to your financial institution to have the over-contribution withdrawn without withholding tax. However, this may take some time, and the penalty clock will keep ticking until the money comes out. So if it were my decision, I'd just take out the over-contribution, eat the withholding tax, and settle up on my next tax return.

 GAIL'S TIPS

• •

If you didn't make your RRSP or TFSA contribution last year, you can catch up. Any RRSP/TFSA room you have from previous years is still yours, and you can catch it up whenever you'd like. You can find the exact amount you can contribute to your RRSP on the Notice of Assessment you receive from the Tax Man each year. This is the notice that comes after you've filed your taxes, which tells you whether they agreed or disagreed with your math. Have a look at the very bottom and you'll see your RRSP Deduction Limit Statement, which will clearly state what your next year's deduction limit will be.

• •

Understand How a Spousal Plan Works

Since the Tax Man recognizes common-law and same-sex relationships for the purposes of contributing to an RRSP or TFSA, I'm going to use the term "partner" instead of "spouse."

Contributions made to an RRSP or a TFSA on behalf of a partner are treated completely differently. The TFSA is simple and straightforward: You can give your partner money to invest in a TFSA without the income generated being attributed back to you and taxed in your hands (since the income is earned tax-free). So you can income split without any tax ramifications.

 GAIL'S TIPS

• •

A TFSA or RRSP belongs to the plan owner—the person in whose name the plan in registered—regardless of who made the contributions. Only the plan owner can make investment decisions or withdrawals from the plan.

If anyone tells you that it's okay to make your own contribution to your spousal plan because it's all the same thing anyway, they're wrong. Don't do it. The Tax Man doesn't care who told you it was okay, it is you who will be held accountable.

• •

Contributions made to a Spousal RRSP are a whole other ball of wax. Usually, the higher-income earner contributes for the lower-income earner and gets the tax deduction, but not always.

Sometimes a partner who has a great pension plan will contribute to a spousal plan for a partner who has no company plan.

One partner can contribute as much as he or she wants to the other's Spousal RRSP, as long as the contributor doesn't go over his or her own contribution limit for the year. So let's say Chris was making a contribution to an RRSP for Sam, and Chris had a contribution limit of $10,000. Chris could put the whole $10K in Sam's Spousal RRSP. Or Chris could put $4,000 in Sam's plan and keep the other $6,000. Chris can divvy up the money in any way that works best for Chris and Sam. Whatever Chris chooses, Chris will get the deduction, but the amount that goes into Sam's RRSP will belong to Sam.

Just because Chris makes a contribution for Sam doesn't mean Sam can't make a contribution. Since Sam's contribution would be based on Sam's income, the Spousal RRSP doesn't affect the individual RRSP contribution limit in any way.

So why would Chris make a contribution to Sam's RRSP, effectively giving up control over the money? Here come those tax benefits again!

Spousal RRSPs are one of the best ways Canadians have to income split—a tax term for making sure the family unit pays the lowest amount of tax possible. Since both Sam and Chris will have independent retirement incomes, they can reduce the likelihood of one person paying a whack of tax while the other person pays next to nothing. Having individual sources of income means each is eligible for the non-refundable tax credit at age 65. It can help avoid the Old Age Security clawback. It may help avoid the age tax credit clawback. And if one partner is younger than the other, it can let the family unit continue to contribute to an RRSP even if it is the older partner who has earned income or undeducted contributions carried forward from a previous year.

Most people assume that Spousal RRSP contributions should always be made by the higher-income partner for the lower-income partner. This is another of those rules to which I say, "Phooey!" How you choose to use a Spousal RRSP depends on what YOU want to achieve.

As I mentioned earlier, if your partner has an excellent pension plan and you have no pension plan, it may make sense for your partner to contribute whatever RRSP contribution they are entitled to make to a plan for you. The idea is to create pretty even incomes come retirement. If your partner earns more but your RRSP is much larger because you started investing earlier or made larger contributions, again the idea is to even out the amount you each have. You may decide to make contributions for your partner. Ditto if your partner earns more now, but plans to take time off to raise kids or go back to school.

Relationship Breakdown

If you're worried about your partner dashing off with your money in the event of the dissolution of your relationship, don't. He or she can wander off with your money regardless of whether you use a spousal plan or not. While the assets in a spousal plan belong to the plan holder, under family law assets belong to both spouses and are equalized—split fairly—in the event of a relationship breakdown.

Transfers between RRSPs due to relationship breakdown have no effect on future contributions.

TFSAs are more complex. If you give some or all of your TFSA funds to your ex due to a divorce/separation agreement, you'll lose the accumulation room you've built up since the launch of TFSAs. The transferred amount will not be added back into your contribution room.

 GAIL'S TIPS

• •

If you withdraw assets from the TFSA before giving the funds to your ex, then the amount of the withdrawal will be added back to your contribution room the following year, so you can keep the contribution room you've built up. Your partner will be able to put those funds into their own TFSA providing they have sufficient contribution room.

• •

Taking Money Out
Withdrawals are one of the areas where RRSPs and TFSAs differ big-time.

Withdrawing money from a TFSA increases your next year's contribution limit by the amount withdrawn. Let's say you made a $5,000 contribution to your TFSA last year. Facing a crimp in your cash flow this year, you take out $3,000. Your contribution room for next year will be the regular room plus the $3,000 you took out, so you can catch up your savings. This is one of the best features of a TFSA.

If you make a withdrawal from your RRSP, you can't put

the money back, and you lose that contribution room forever.

If you make a withdrawal from a Spousal RRSP, special rules apply. See page 291.

The Debate

I think the great shame is that we expect a winner in the TFSA/ RRSP tournament of champions. While the TFSA is a terrific product, it doesn't take the place of an RRSP, particularly for people who are 40 and younger or those who are in a high income tax bracket. And if we make it an either/or question, someone has to lose. I think it will be the contributor.

No doubt the government would love it if we turned our backs on RRSPs in favour of the TFSA. Since the TFSA has no tax deferral on contributions, the government doesn't have to give you back your hard-earned tax dollars when you choose a TFSA over an RRSP. Sure, it grows on a tax-free basis, and that's great. But it isn't a patch on the income the government would have to give up if everyone started making the maximum RRSP contribution every year.

As with everything else to do with money, the decision to choose one plan over another depends on your marginal tax rate when you're putting the money in and when you're taking the money out. And it depends on what you do with the tax savings you derive from having contributed to an RRSP.

Since TFSA contribution room isn't affected by existing pension contributions, anyone who belongs to a company pension plan may want to take a good hard look at the TFSA as an option to an RRSP.

Unless, of course, you're already using your TFSA as your

emergency fund. This is, perhaps, my favourite use for a TFSA: to build up and manage an emergency fund. It's the perfect product since whatever money you take out one year can be put back in without affecting a future year's contribution.

If you're still building your emergency fund and you're under 40, consider using an RRSP to grow your retirement savings for as long as it takes to maximize your emergency fund. Once your emergency fund is up to where you want it to be, if you're earning income that has you paying tax at 35% or less, maximize your TFSA first and then put any additional savings in your RRSP.

 GAIL'S TIPS

• •

Everyone should have an emergency fund to take care of those times when your income goes down or completely evaporates due to a downturn in the economy, personal stress, or ill health. The general rule of thumb is to have enough cash to cover six months' worth of essential expenses, so that if the worst does happen, you have some money to help ride out the emergency. Having an emergency fund also means you'll be less likely to tap your long-term savings to deal with short-term financial challenges.

• •

If you are in the top tax brackets so that you're paying more than 35% in tax, use an RRSP to maximize your retirement savings and to manage your tax liability. Use the TFSA for emergency savings, for pools of money that must accumulate like a home maintenance fund, and to top up your retirement savings.

If you're over 50 and have never used an RRSP, you won't have as much time to put the tax-deferred compounding of an RRSP on your side. Unless you're in the very top two tax brackets and will get a whack of cash back from the Tax Man now (a bird in the hand), stick with a TFSA.

If you're beyond the age where you can contribute to an RRSP (71), use a TFSA to shelter the income you're earning on your investments since any income earned in a TFSA is earned tax-free.

Besides immediate and future tax savings, the other factor that will impact your decision to use a TFSA or an RRSP as your first choice for retirement savings is how you put the tax savings you'll get from an RRSP to work. Since saving on income tax is a driving force behind many Canadians' decision to contribute to an RRSP, how you use those tax savings is something you should think about.

- Will you use the savings on your taxes to boost your future RRSP contributions?
- Will you use the tax savings you get to pay off consumer debt or pay down your mortgage?
- Will you re-incorporate your tax savings into cash flow so you can take a holiday or pay for your kids' hockey fees?

Don't give short shrift to what you'll do with your tax savings if you decide to go with an RRSP. Being able to stash away some cash for the future AND take a lovely vacation using your tax refund may be all the motivation you need to set up your automatic savings plan. Ditto the satisfaction of knowing that you have locked and loaded your retirement savings for the year, resulting in a tidy tax refund you can use as a mortgage prepayment. Hey, whatever floats your boat. Just don't forget that the way to achieve any goal is to take some action.

To sum up:

Pro TFSA

1. If you have a low income now and/or you expect to have a low income when you retire, and you are concerned about your eligibility for government benefits like OAS or GIS, maximize your TFSA before using an RRSP so you can access your savings without triggering more tax on your income.

2. If you think you may need to tap the money—noooooo!—use a TFSA since the contribution room is restored after a withdrawal, which it isn't if you take money out of your RRSP.

3. If you will be in a higher tax bracket when you retire and are concerned about paying a lot of tax when you pull the money out of the RRSP, use a TFSA.

4. If you're pretty close to retirement—15 years or closer—and you're going to be using fixed income investments, use a TFSA.

5. If you're over the age of 71 and you're still saving (really?), use a TFSA.

6. If you want to use your RRSP for your own retirement savings, but still want to help your mate save, you can contribute to a TFSA for your mate without affecting your own TFSA limit and there's no tax implication for you.

7. If you think it is likely that you'll die early (again, really?) and leave a stash of cash behind to anyone other than a spouse, a TFSA will get better tax treatment than an RRSP, so stick with a TFSA.

Pro RRSP

1. If you are in a high tax bracket now (or expect to be because of your career choice) and are concerned about minimizing the amount of money you're giving to the Tax Man, use an RRSP. You can then use your tax refund to build up your TFSA or pay down your mortgage and you'll be ahead of the game even if your marginal tax rate remains high at retirement.

2. If you think your tax rate will be lower at retirement, use an RRSP.

3. If your savings exceed the TFSA limit, use an RRSP.

4. If you're using all your TFSA room for your emergency savings, use an RRSP for retirement savings.

5. If you're planning to buy a home and want to take advantage of the RRSP Home Buyers' Plan, use an RRSP.

6. If you think you may be returning to school and want to take advantage of the RRSP Lifelong Learning Plan, use an RRSP.

7. If you want to make sure that both you and your spouse have similar amounts of pension income so both you and your partner will have enough to claim the pension income deduction, use an RRSP for at least a portion of your savings.

8. If you're under the age of 18 when you start to save, use an RRSP.

Okay, so now you know whether you're better suited to an RRSP or to a TFSA for your retirement savings. I've also tried to give you as much information as I can to create your own plan. But if your situation is complicated, or if you're feeling overwhelmed, you may want to consider finding someone to guide you, teach you, be your sounding board as you move forward.

WHO TO ASK FOR HELP

The financial world is filled with an alphabet soup of designations for people who purport to be available to help you. Sometimes, however, these people are only working to help their companies or themselves. You must be very careful in making your choices.

Here are some of the most common designations you'll come across in increasing order of helpfulness and education, and how they may be able to help you:

- **PFP** stands for Personal Financial Planner, which is a designation created by the chartered banks to add credibility for their staff. PFPs must complete courses in personal financial counselling, insurance, estate planning, and taxation. However, I've met more than a few people with this designation who didn't understand some of the most basic rules despite having completed the training.
- **CFP** stands for Certified Financial Planner. This designation is recognized in 14 countries around the world. To

become a CFP, a body must have successfully completed an accredited educational program (or hold specific professional and educational designations), pass the national exam, and have a minimum of two years' relevant work experience. CFPs must adhere to a professional code of ethics and must complete 30 hours of continuing education every year.

- **RFP** stands for Registered Financial Planner, which is an advanced financial planning designation that requires holders to demonstrate their ability to apply their knowledge in the completion of a comprehensive financial plan. Like CFPs, RFPs are subject to annual continuing education requirements and a code of professional ethics. They must also carry professional liability insurance.

Your next decision will affect your wallet: You can go "no fee" or "fee only."

When you work with a fee-only financial planner, you'll pay an hourly or package fee for the advice you receive. Since they do not make money by selling products, these advisors should be focused on trying to help you sort out what it is YOU want. If you hit a body who seems to be pushing you in a direction you don't like or offering options you don't understand, cut your losses in terms of the time invested and move on. (Back in March 2008, *MoneySense* magazine created a list of fee-only financial planners you might want to check out.)

When you work with someone who is selling products and earning a commission, you will likely not be charged a fee, but you will have to buy the products and services sold by that individual/financial company. This usually means a more limited range of options.

Whomever you choose, this person should be willing and able to refer you to specialists in a variety of arenas, not all of whom work for their organization (because if they do it isn't a "referral," it's "cross-selling"). For example, if you need help with tax issues, if you want to create an estate plan, or if you need insurance, your financial planner should have experts with whom they work regularly and to whom they can refer you. If your financial planner can't provide you with a list of resources without "checking" first, run for the hills. Most are well connected and work on the "I'll scratch your back if you scratch mine" referral system, so they have each other's names at their fingertips.

If you're looking for someone with whom you can forge a long-term relationship, start by narrowing your prospective list of candidates to about three or four. Ask friends, family, colleagues, and business associates for the names of the people with whom they deal. Ask your accountant. Ask your lawyer. You might also want to take some courses on money taught by financial experts to see if there's someone whose approach you really like. Read the paper and see who is writing the expert articles and who is being quoted.

Once you narrow your list down, check your candidate's credentials and references. Check with your regional licensing bodies like a Securities Commission or Insurance Commission to see if any complaints have been registered against any of the bodies you are considering.

Now it's time to interview your short list. A face-to-face will go a long way in helping you get a sense of the person. Will you be comfortable working with this person? Do you like his manner? Do you like her communication style? Finding an advisor whom you respect and trust, and with whom you will enjoy working, is important if you want to have confidence in their recommendations.

Be upfront about the fact that you are evaluating several candidates and that you hope to make a decision soon. Expect your candidates to ask you questions too. They'll want to know your priorities in terms of the financial goals you're hoping to accomplish, along with your expectations, and how you'd like to work with them.

While horror stories abound about advisors who don't know their stuff and who don't take their fiduciary responsibilities seriously, there are some very good advisors out there. In my opinion, your best bet will be to focus on those who work on a fee-only basis and are willing to draw you up a plan on paper. I think you should avoid anyone with an affiliation in the mutual funds industry since many employees are bound to sell their employer's funds . . . often with sales targets that have them churning their clients' portfolios. And when you're asking for references, make sure you say, "I'd like one of the three references you give me to be someone very much like me."

Questions to Ask Advisors

How will you help me establish my goals and
    determine my best course of action?
How long have you worked with your most long-lived
    client?

Do you only provide direction or can you also help me
with implementation?

What are your areas of expertise?

What are your greatest strengths?

What are your greatest weaknesses?

What ongoing training and education have you
received?

Tell me about the team with which you work for
things such as estate planning, tax counselling,
and investment management?

Do you have a team of professionals such as lawyers,
accountants, and insurance specialists with whom
you work?

What financial products are you licensed to sell?

Are you limited to selling products for certain
companies?

How are you paid?

What is YOUR investment philosophy?

What information will you provide to me to support
your recommendations?

How often will you contact me, and how?

Questions to Ask References

How long have you worked with this advisor?

Are you happy with the services you've been receiving?

What are this advisor's strong points?

What are this advisor's weak points?

What have you been disappointed or surprised by in your
relationship?

How often do you hear from your advisor?

Who normally initiates the calls, and for what reason?

How quickly are your calls returned?

What is it that you really value about your relationship
with your advisor?

Finding a body with whom you are comfortable can take a lot of work off your plate. And knowing that you have someone who is watching your money on a day-to-day basis means you can pay attention to other things. But it doesn't mean you can totally give over the control and the decision-making. A lot of fools have done that and then cried about how they were "taken." Your advisor is only that: an advisor. It's still your money. And you have the most to lose or win. So keep your eye on the ball.

TIME TO ACT

Time for some action. You've been sitting at home, comfy and safe, working through the process with me. You've figured out how much you are saving and how much more you need to save. You've also figured out how to put those savings to work using investments that match your time horizon and your investment risk tolerance. And you now know whether you'll be using an RRSP or TFSA or some combination of both to take control of your retirement and your future. All that's left is to act.

This may be the hardest part of all.

If you haven't been saving, inertia will hold you riveted to inaction. You'll have to fight like hell to get out of "doing nothing" and into "doing something." I'm here to kick your butt into action, right now.

If you find your mind filling with a dozen reasons why you shouldn't or can't do anything today, that's self-doubt rearing its ugly head. Self-doubt can cripple you. So can your insecurity because you've never done anything like this before. Or it may just be the Dastardly Procrastination Devil that tells you to put it off until next payday.

Don't delay. Act today.

Go online or pick up the phone and make an appointment to set up an automatic deduction from your transaction account to your savings account today.

If you don't have an advisor yet, call your friends and family and find out who they deal with and make some appointments to do some interviewing. Set a deadline for yourself: I will have chosen an advisor by (four weeks from today).

If you aren't knowledgeable about investing, start by using alternatives with which you are comfortable, and then make a commitment to learning more about how you can put your money to work for you. Explore community college night courses, seminars given by local financial institutions, the web.

If, at this point, you choose to do nothing, I'm gonna haunt you. Every time you pull your wallet out to spend a dime, you're going to hear my voice in your head saying, "So, spending money, eh? Where's that retirement plan I worked hard on with you?" Each time you order a pizza, get your hair cut, or buy a cuppa, you'll hear my voice in your head saying, "How much could you have if you saved just half that money?" Every time you flip on the TV, you'll hear my voice in your head saying, "Time to watch TV but no time to open up a TFSA or RRSP? Really?"

All that's standing between you and the future you want is action. You can't use "I don't know" or "I'm not sure" anymore as your excuse. You do know. And even if you're not 100% confident, you have enough information to take action.

Ready?

Set?

Do it!

Having put your plan into action, you're still not quite done. You've charted your course. Now you must steer your boat through waters, smooth and choppy, to get to where you want to be next. That means monitoring and adjusting as your life unfolds. And that's the next part of our journey together.

10

MONITOR AND ADJUST

Once you've started investing, you can't simply close your eyes and hope for the best. Buying an investment, whether it's in an RRSP or a TFSA, is just the first step. Now you have to monitor how those investments are doing and adjust your portfolio as you go.

Your purpose, or how you plan to use the money when you finally do spend it, plays an important part in this monitor-and-adjust stage. While the focus of this book is on taking control of your retirement and your future, people have all sorts of reasons for setting aside some money. But if you're not clear on what it is you are trying to achieve with each pool of money, you can fall into the trap of thinking you're doing a better job of retirement planning than you actually are. And you can royally screw up when it comes to choosing ways to put that money to work to make more money.

There was a time when the only thing an RRSP was used for was saving for retirement. "Never touch this money," the experts expounded. "An RRSP is a long-term investment," The Spurts declared. In reality, people use their RRSPs for a multitude of purposes. Some people dip in to return to school or train for a new career. Couples with families dip in to provide income while home with their tots. People thrown into periods of unemployment dip in to make ends meet. Even the government got into the swing, introducing two perfectly legal ways to dip in without tax consequence: to buy a home or to fund your education.

Building an investment portfolio is only one step in a long journey. Having figured out your risk tolerance, your time horizon, and your investment objectives you've made choices about what to invest in. Now you have to monitor, and make adjustments to, those choices to make sure your investments continue to serve you well.

CREATE AN ONGOING REVIEW PLAN

A twice-a-year review of your investment portfolio is a good idea, but at the very least you should do a complete review once a year to evaluate

- how each investment is doing,
- how your investment time horizon may have changed,
- how your risk profile may have changed, and
- if your asset allocation is still balanced the way you want it to be.

How Are You Doing?

Time changes everything and failing to recognize how things have changed can be pretty hard on your investment portfolio. You need to look at the choices you made in light of what's happening in the here and now. Since, over time, you'll develop more experience and knowledge, you should bring that to bear on your past choices. Ask yourself this question: Would I buy this investment today, knowing what I know now about how things have turned out? If the answer is yes, then you'll likely want to hold on to it. If your answer is no, it may be time to sell.

 GAIL'S TIPS

If you are actively trading your portfolio, you'll want to do a reassessment of your holdings at least on a quarterly basis, comparing data for the current quarter with that of the same quarter a year ago, looking at your investment's growth rate, and ranking your choices in terms of performance.

Since over-trading an investment portfolio is a sure way to blow your brains out on fees, and churning your portfolio goes counter to the sage advice "buy and hold," some investors think they can just close their eyes and pray. But you can't. If you're going to manage your own investment portfolio, you need to take the time to assess and reassess what you're doing right and what you're doing wrong.

If you decide to sell an investment because you believe that it has gone up as much as it's likely to, so there is more downside risk, you'll need to go shopping for a new investment to replace it. Having a phantom portfolio running beside your real one—tracking a bunch of investments you're interested in, but haven't yet bought, either on paper or using a website— can be so handy since you'll have identified investments you like and can turn to these for your next pick.

 GAIL'S TIPS

There are dozens of sites on the web that will let you create an imaginary stock portfolio, track and trade your investments, and develop some skills as an investor. The objective is to make some of those mistakes beginners inevitably make—through ignorance, excitement, or fear—while you're still using pretend money. If you get those first five, 10, or 20 mistakes out of your system—and if you learn from them because you've taken this whole exercise seriously— that's a lot less money you'll lose to the market when you finally do hit that trade button.

If you've invested in mutual funds, performance isn't the only thing to look at. Has your fund manager changed? If so, how has it affected your fund? If your last few years have been great, but the manager who produced those returns has just gone to a new fund, will your fund continue to do well under the new manager? You'll have to check the new manager's track record, if there is one, to see if you like how they do things.

Have the expenses on the fund changed? Don't just assume the fees you're used to will remain the same. Quantify how much the fund is charging in fees and how that's impacting your return.

Have the goals of the fund changed? Mutual funds are notorious for changing their direction midstream. A "Japanese" fund becomes an "Asian" fund. A small-cap fund that's taken on lots of new investment dollars is forced to broaden its investment scope. Again, life changes, and so do mutual funds' goals. Are you still happy with them, or is it time to move on?

Time Horizon

No matter how far away your retirement plans, at some point before you hang up your spurs you have to adjust to a medium-term and then a short-term investment horizon. That means moving from alternatives like stocks to medium-term bonds, then short-term deposits, and eventually, cash. Whether you pool all the money together in a single investment plan, or you keep the pools separate, it's a good idea to put a timeline on the front of your file folder as a reminder about remixing your assets as your time horizon shortens.

Risk Profile

Have any major life changes occurred since your last portfolio review? If you have gotten married, had a child, bought a house, or changed jobs, these changes could have an impact on your risk tolerance. So, too, could getting a divorce, having a kid go off to university, or becoming widowed.

Experience and knowledge may also change your risk profile. As you become more comfortable with different types of investments, you may find you're more willing to look at options you wouldn't have even considered before.

Doing a risk assessment like the ones on pages 149 to 156 takes very little time. And it's time well spent if it means you're a better decision-maker. You should do a new risk profile at least once every two years.

Asset Allocation

As some of your investments outperform others, your asset mix will change. So that ABC Fund you bought that made up 15% of your portfolio has grown by leaps and bounds (lucky you) and now makes up 28% of your portfolio. Are you going to go with the higher exposure to that fund, or do you want to sell of some of those units and rebalance your portfolio to keep your asset mix in line. You'll have to look at how the various classes of investments (fixed income, growth, speculative, etc.) have changed and decide if your asset allocation needs to be rebalanced.

CH...CH...CH...CHANGES

No matter how well planned your life has been, there are myriad life events that will come along and force you to reassess your priorities and take stock of where you are. Some are events for which you carefully planned—or thought you did— like having a baby. Others will broadside you, pushing you off the Savings Road. Still others will make you dance a jig. Never take the Ups for granted, and know that each Down has an important lesson that will prepare you for something else in your life. Regardless of whether your change brings an up or down, that change will likely have an impact on your financial life and the perfect plan you created. Here's how to deal with those changes when they come along.

You're Home with Your Wee One

Loads of people have let the idea of maternity benefits lull them in to thinking that the money is taken care of. Often those people are surprised to learn how little Employment Insurance (EI) pays. They use credit to fill the money gap at maternity and end up deeply in the hole. They go back to work, earning enough to rebalance their budgets. But with a whack of debt to repay, they feel squeezed and their competing priorities inevitably mean they sacrifice their savings.

Sure you can catch up later. Well, you can catch up the contributions, but not the time. And that's the fly in the ointment. If you haven't already established a healthy savings pool that can continue to expand even when you're not contributing, you're hardly in a position to stop saving.

Assuming you had some foresight and started saving for retirement early enough, you could put a hold on your long-term savings until you're back to work. Of course, if you're barely making ends meet, this may be your only option. In this case, know that this is just a break, and plan for what will come next: increased savings, seeking a higher return on your investments, contributing for longer.

 **GAIL'S TIPS**

. . . .

If you find your income reduced for the year you're on maternity leave, you'll also see your marginal tax rate go down. Claiming a deduction for an RRSP contribution would mean frittering away a perfectly good deduction on a low-income year. Better to hold the deduction for a year when your taxable income is back up. Most people don't realize that you can make a contribution and not claim it, holding the deduction for a year when it will be more beneficial tax-wise.

In the year you return to work, your contribution room will be lower because it's calculated on your previous year's earned income—when you were home with baby. So you'll have less room to manoeuvre when trying to minimize your taxes. But wait, you still have that un-deducted contribution from the previous year, and it will come in very handy in reducing your taxes.

Knowing you can delay claiming your deduction without losing it means you can plan to make those RRSP contributions work even harder in terms of the deduction you'll eventually receive. It also eliminates the excuse, "What's the point, I don't pay that much tax now anyway."

. . . .

You see, it's all about choices. There are lots of ways to get to the same end. You just have to find the means that works best for you.

What you should not do is assume that everything will be fine and blithely ignore your future. And no matter how much you want to save for your new baby's education, that should not take precedence over your own retirement savings. Sure, you can do a little of both. But not using these prime compounding years to build up a nest egg can be a mistake.

Whether you stay home with baby for three months, a year, or a long, long time, stay conscious of the fact that whatever time you give up now in terms of growing your savings may mean more time on the other end: delaying retirement. As long as you're making a conscious choice, the choice is yours to make. Choose to live in the land of delusion and ignorance and that too is a choice.

You Lose Your Job

Job loss comes with two big stressors. First, there is the financial stuff that you need to figure out. Second, there is the emotional misery that you must wade through. Either piles of poop can sink you, so above all else, it is very, very important that you keep a cool head.

Your first instinct might be to tap your RRSP for the money you'll need to keep living like you did while you were working. Resist the urge. Whatever you take out of your RRSP now can't be put back in. You lose that contribution room. Forever.

Learning to live on less while you're unemployed is part of being unemployed. If you pretend nothing much has changed, you'll get to the end with your reserves depleted and no resources for the future.

If you're living on EI benefits, you likely don't have a red cent left over to save. Don't sweat it. You'll get back to saving when you get back on your feet. In the mean time, make sure you're doing everything possible to reduce your expenses. Your objective should be to live within your means so you're not racking up debt that can affect your ability to save later on. As for what you need to know about how to deal with your company pension plan, read on.

You Change Jobs

When you change jobs, you are entitled to all the money you put into your pension plan plus any return you earned on those assets. After a certain period (determined by provincial legislation), you are also entitled to your employer's contributions. This is called being "vested." Once your pension vests, all your employer's contributions become yours.

You have five choices as to what to do with your pension:

1. Leave it where it is.
2. Move it to your new plan, assuming there is one.
3. Buy an annuity.
4. Transfer your pension to a locked-in retirement account, or LIRA.
5. Take the cash and run (but you'll pay a whack of tax).

There are pros and cons to each option, and there can be some pretty complicated math that goes along with options one and two, so you'd be wise to go see your benefits administrator and have a thorough discussion about the upsides and downsides before moving your money.

How much you'll receive if the pension is vested and funds are transferred out depends on the type of pension plan you have. With a DBP, the eligible amount—referred to as the "commuted value"—is calculated based on the formula used to calculate what you're entitled to, and predictions of future value. So it will depend on how long you've been part of the plan and the number of years left to your retirement date. DBP values grow slowly in your early working years, picking up speed in mid-career. The further away you are from that date, the less you'll get.

As long as the funds remain in either a company pension plan or LIRA, no taxes are payable on your pension assets when you move from one job to the next. However, you may receive a pension adjustment reversal (PAR), which creates a one-time boost in the amount you can contribute to your RRSP. And if you receive a retiring allowance, you may be able to take advantage of a special tax-free rollover if you contribute some or all of the allowance to your RRSP. Again, speak with your benefits administrator; get the facts and save on tax.

 **GAIL'S TIPS**

• •

A retiring allowance is often called "severance pay" and is paid when you retire in recognition of your long service, or when you're terminated. The amount of your retiring allowance that you may transfer to your RRSP is limited. You're allowed to transfer

- $2,000 for each year or part of a year before 1996
- $1,500 for each year or part of a year before 1989

If you became employed after 1996, you're not entitled to roll over any of your severance or retiring allowance.

• •

If you haven't built up much in the way of assets, transferring your DBP to a new DBP might allow you to continue to build up years of service in order to qualify for your maximum pension. Having a bunch of little pensions scattered all over the place may do you no good at all. However, deciding to transfer your DBP to a LIRA could result in the loss of other employer benefits like extended health care, dental care, or pension increases that offset inflation. So get the facts before you make your choice.

With a defined contribution plan (DCP), the amount is straightforward: It's the combined employee/employer contributions plus investment returns. There will be restrictions on what you can do with the money. You'll likely have to move the money to a LIRA and stick with specific investments. You may also be restricted from tapping into your cash before retirement age.

If you had a group RRSP, you're subject to regular RRSP rules. You can transfer your money to another RRSP with no tax implications, but the money is taxable if you cash it out.

When it comes to making this decision, it's a matter of looking at the numbers and doing the math. You'll need your benefits administrator's assistance in working out the figures and deciding what will work best for you, given your pension plan and personal circumstances. There is no one right or wrong answer. As with so many other things to do with money, it depends. Make some cookies and go woo your benefits administrator.

You Get Sick

Getting sick sucks. And if your illness stops you from working completely, it can throw the best-laid plans completely off track. Don't despair. You may be able to receive benefits from your pension plan or qualify for disability payments from CPP. Make a call to your benefits administrator to see whether

- your DBP offers a disability pension and allows you to continue to earn credits towards your pension even though you've stopped working. If it does, when you reach your normal retirement age, your regular pension payments would start.
- because you're in a DCP and receive payments from a workplace disability program, you're still considered an employee. If so, you won't be able to take money from your retirement savings. But your employer may continue to contribute to your pension until you retire.
- because you have a group RRSP at work, you can withdraw money at any time as long as your employer agrees. Careful though, since taking money out of your retirement

savings will move you further away from your goal of having a financially secure retirement. That being said, if you don't have any other means of supporting yourself while you are ill, getting some dough will be your first priority.

 GAIL'S TIPS

. . . .

If you are living on a significantly reduced income—be it because of illness, layoff, maternity, whatever—you may be upset because you cannot save. I'm sorry you are in a tough spot and I wish there were some magic wand I could wave to make it all better. There isn't. Hopefully you've heeded my advice and have an emergency fund and enough of the right kind of insurance to see you through. If you haven't, then your retirement savings will no doubt take a back seat to coping with your illness and your smaller income.

There is no magic to saving. The only way to have money in the future is to not spend all the money you get today. If you get so little that it takes all of it to keep body and soul together, then saving isn't an option. There's nothing I can tell you that will fix the problem of "no money."

If you feel you must save because you don't like the idea of not saving, then you may get creative: taking in a roommate and banking their share of the rent, for example. But only you know what you are able to do given your situation and your desired outcome. Some people don't mind sharing their space. Others would rather eat noodles five days a week to keep their privacy. Only you can know what will work for you. But if you have no extra money, wringing your hands and twisting in the wind won't make you have a better life. Get busy making the very best life you can working with the cards you've been dealt.

• •

You're Making Less Money

Every time there is a downturn in the economy and people have their hours cut back, the first thing that suffers is the savings. I get that adjusting to a reduced income is tough. And I get that it makes no sense to go into debt to "save." What I don't buy at all is the way people who used to make more money and now don't believe this excuses them from having to prepare for the future. Really? Because you're never going to retire?

While it may take you a few weeks or even a few months to get a handle on your expenses and come up with the money you need to save, that should be one of your goals. After all, if you save nothing now, you'll have nothing in the future.

Learning to manage on less money means you have some choices to make. Your housing costs may be out of whack, and downsizing or moving to a less expensive area may be your solution. You'll likely have to cut back on eating out, drive your car a little longer, and learn to bargain shop for clothes for the kids. Focusing on the joy of "more time" may let you see the bright side of the picture. And if you're willing to think outside the box you can create new ways of making money.

Life offers no guarantees. The key is to be flexible and willing to make choices that are different from the ones with which you may have become very familiar. All the while you have to stay focused on making sure you have something for the future. If you think it's hard living on less money now, what'll it be like at retirement if you have nothing saved?

Your Income Goes Up

Yippee! You're making more money. Before you rush out and find 92 ways to spend your raise, think for a minute. Have you figured out how much more money you'll be saving because you're now making more money? Regardless of what percentage of your income you were saving, the amount you're setting aside every month just went up. Have you adjusted your automatic savings to reflect the higher amount?

 GAIL'S TIPS

• •

Since a raise may also come with a bigger tax bite, you may also want to look at whether your choice of TFSA over RRSP still holds water.

• •

You might even decide that with this new raise you can afford to save a larger percentage to build up a bigger nest egg. This will be particularly true if you've suffered some interruptions in your savings, like unemployment or maternity leave. Will you move from saving 10% to saving 11%? It doesn't have to be a huge step up. Every little bit counts. You might even decide to live on your pre-raise income and ramp up your savings. Hey, it's your money. They are your goals.

What you shouldn't do is ignore the fact that more money means you have more money to save and let lifestyle inflation eat your raise.

 GAIL'S TIPS

Lifestyle inflation is something that happens naturally to people as their incomes go up. You move into a nice neighbourhood. Everyone is driving new-model cars. You feel the pressure to upgrade your clunker. It's called peer pressure or keeping up with the Joneses, and it's insidious.

There is nothing wrong with giving your quality of life a boost when you start making more money. You should enjoy the lifestyle that you're working so hard for. But it's just as important that you give your goals a nod by reviewing them, and perhaps setting some new ones. Make sure you keep a piece of all the new money you're making by upping your auto-savings so you are socking away more for the future.

Spending more money consciously to have a more satisfying life is fine. Simply reacting to the fact that we're feeling richer by blowing gobs of dough on crap is stupid. If you let lifestyle inflation drive your spending, you'll rue it the next time you have a setback. Those $600 shoes will look like a pretty dumb move when you're staring into your empty fridge.

You Get a Divorce

One of the things you'll have to deal with if your marriage breaks down is the sharing of property: your home, your stuff, your savings. When the asset being valued is a pension, valuation can become particularly icky. If your province considers the pension to be a family asset, it must be valued and divided like other family assets.

Splitting Pension Assets

If you have a DCP, group RRSP, or individual RRSP, the calculation is straightforward. However, if you or your spouse has a DBP, this can be a phenomenally complicated, and often expensive, task. Since the amount to be divided must only be the amount accumulated during the marriage, the entire pension will very likely not be split. Valuators and accountants must then be brought in to consider the method of calculation, mortality tables, early retirement provisions, death benefits, and tax consequences.

If it's your DBP being split, you will want to ensure that your pension is valued as low as you can legally justify. If it's the other guy's pension, then you have to be aware that this is the tact they will take. Ask for an independent pension valuation so you don't end up walking away from thousands in assets.

Depending on what province you live in, one of these three things could happen:

1. You make a trade. Your ex agrees to let you keep your pension and takes something else of equal value, like the house.
2. You divide it up now. You and your ex agree to split the pension. Your plan transfers your ex-spouse's share to his or her RRSP, assuming your plan allows this.
3. You split the pension later when you retire. The plan will pay part of the pension to you and part to your ex-spouse. It's up to each of you to make sure you get your fair share.

 GAIL'S TIPS

Choosing to keep the family home and giving up retirement assets in exchange isn't always a smart move. If you have stayed out of the workforce to raise a family or have had lower paying jobs, you may want to hold on to at least a portion of the family's retirement assets. You'll be starting from ground zero if you relinquish RRSP assets totally. This is particularly important if you are in your late 40s or 50s and have less time to rebuild a strong retirement asset base.

During separation or divorce, you can transfer existing RRSPs to your ex without being subject to tax as long as you are living apart when property and assets are settled and you have a written separation agreement or a court order.

A 50–50 split of RRSP assets may seem fair. However, your partner may have significant unused RRSP contribution room. Those catch-up contributions aren't divisible after the settlement. Negotiate for a portion of those contributions to be made in your name (as a spousal contribution) prior to the division of assets, and make sure that the Spousal RRSP will not be equalized. That way you'll have assets that can continue to grow on a tax-deferred basis.

Once you are living separately, the RRSP rules for withdrawals from a spousal plan change. The money taken from a spousal plan will be taxed in the plan holder's hands. So don't go grabbing money out of your spousal plan thinking your old buddy will get stuck with the tax bill. You'll end up paying the piper.

Splitting Canada Pension Plan Credits

Canada Pension Plan pension credits can also be divided. This division is called "credit splitting." The credits of both spouses are added together for the time they lived together and the total number of credits is divided equally between them. These credits are not actually paid. They are used to determine the amount of any CPP benefits to which you may be entitled.

Credits can be split even if one partner did not pay into CPP. The longer you and your ex were together, and the bigger the difference between your earnings while you were together, the greater the exchange of credits will be. Splitting credits works to your advantage if you were the lower wage earner since it would increase your CPP credits, giving you a larger pension when you retire.

Canada Pension Plan splits only the credits for the time you cohabited, and works in calendar years. In calculating a credit split, CPP includes the whole calendar year for the year you began living together, but does not include any of the calendar year for the year the relationship ended.

To apply for credit splitting, you must provide originals or certified copies of your marriage certificate, proof of divorce or legal annulment court documents, and any separation agreements and/or Minutes of Settlement between you and your former spouse. In the case of a common-law relationship, you'll be asked to make a Statutory Declaration to establish the length of a common-law relationship.

Now that you're on your own and responsible for taking care of your own future, go back to Part 1 of this book and recalculate your net worth. This will give you a good idea of what you'll need to focus on as you move forward.

Your Partner Dies

Partners die. Sometimes it happens suddenly. Sometimes it is after years of illness and suffering. Regardless, it feels like in a split second everything about your life has changed. Often it doesn't take very long for the focus to shift from grief to worry as the financial challenges start to rear their ugly heads.

Once you've had time to take stock of your financial reality—a mortgage to be paid, insurance benefits that can be used to provide an income or pay off debt, an income to be generated—you'll have to eventually come back to the question of what you're going to do to plan for the future.

You have to go back to Part 1 of this book. Recalculate what you own and what you owe and figure out your net worth. This will give you a snapshot of what you'll need to focus on as you move forward.

If your partner had RRSP assets, they can be transferred to your RRSP without tax consequence through your partner's beneficiary designation or will. You won't have to pay any tax on the money, provided you roll the funds directly into your own retirement savings. And this rollover won't use up your contribution room. You may also be entitled to a lump sum from the corporate pension plan, which can be transferred tax-free to an RRSP in your name, so check with your partner's employer.

If your partner had a defined benefit plan, your payments would be based on the pension benefits your honey earned before death depending on the rules of the plan. It may be paid to you in a lump sum or as regular pension when you retire. Check with the pension plan administrator to see how it will work. Some plans pay a percentage of the full pension to a surviving spouse, but this will vary from one DBP to another.

If your partner had a defined contribution plan, as the beneficiary you'll get all the money in the account.

Now that you're on your own, without a pal as a backup, you're going to be fully responsible for yourself, including your retirement savings. You may have banked on sharing your retirement expenses with your buddy. Now you'll have to make a new plan. The early days will be the toughest. As time goes by, the fog will clear and you'll see your way to setting new goals. Give yourself some time to adapt to your new status and then make a plan.

Your Partner Won't Save

We can love a body without ever understanding what makes that body tick. Even couples that have been together for eons scratch their heads at some of the things their mates do. That's because we are evolving creatures constantly responding to the stimuli around us, constantly growing, constantly changing. Well, some of us.

Sometimes folks end up in relationships where they are very badly matched financially. You're a saver. Your partner is a spender. You think about the future. Your partner lives for today. You're conservative. Your partner likes to take risks.

If you're counting on your buddy to do the things you need to do to keep your financial boat afloat and they don't, you may have to accept that you're in this ship alone. If you are living with a partner who is irresponsible with money, you have three choices:

1. You can stay, living life on the rollercoaster and hoping for the best.
2. You can leave, uprooting everyone and bearing the cost of the breakup both financially and emotionally—so you better be dead sure that this is the right step.
3. You can accept that you can't change your mate, stop your whining, and create a protective wall that isolates your partner's aberrant behaviour and keeps your family safe.

Whether your partner gambles, drinks, does drugs, uses credit like it's never going to run out, likes to change their vehicle every six months, can't walk past a store without dropping a bundle, or just won't save a dime, if you've begged, pleaded, cried, threatened, and even tried to walk away, maybe it's time to accept that this is who your partner is. If you love your mate, it may mean accepting them for who they are and getting on with the business of life.

If you can't live with it, you know what you must do. If you can't live without it, but don't want their storms to sink your ship, it's time to take some steps to protect yourself and your family.

Make sure you are not on the hook for any of your partner's borrowing. That means no joint credit. No co-signing. No sharing of credit cards or bank accounts (keep your cards and your PINs to yourself) especially where overdraft protection may leave you on the hook.

If you own a home together, accept that your home may not be around forever. Any joint assets will be at risk since if your partner ends up in bankruptcy, those assets will be part of the proceedings. The only way to avoid this is if your partner's name is not on title. If it is, paying down your mortgage may be an exercise in frustration, since whatever assets you build up may be affected by your partner's wanton spending and rampant debt.

Save/invest separately. Ha! Who are we kidding? Your partner isn't saving. Just make sure they don't know where the money is or have any access to it. It doesn't exist as far as they're concerned.

Come up with a plan for the expenses. Your partner has to give you a specific amount every week to meet the family's needs. If they don't, then you're stuck with a freeloader and should reconsider your options. If they do, that money goes into an account that you use to make sure the essential bills are paid. The other stuff can be paid from their own account.

Yup, you've got separate accounts! And now that you're sharing expenses fairly, you've got some money to save for your own future.

Keep your hand out of your pocket. This is the toughest thing you'll have to do. You cannot save your partner. You should not attempt to rescue them when the tears start. It's part of the condition. You have to grit your teeth and NOT bite the hook. If you fail at this part, you'll fail altogether!

This isn't about punishing your partner. It's about protecting yourself. And if you have children, they need your protection. Just because one member of your team can't see beyond their own nose doesn't mean the whole family should suffer. If you've got a partner who just doesn't get it, you've got a rough road to walk. I've been there and you have my sympathies.

You Must Declare Personal Bankruptcy

The web is full of inaccurate information when it comes to what will happen to your pension savings if you file for bankruptcy. That's because the rules changed and loads of sites haven't yet updated their info. (This is one of the big downsides to the Internet . . . old crap lives on for-frickin'-ever.) Here are the facts: Effective July 7, 2008, all RRSPs, RRIFs, and DPSPs are now exempt from seizure in a bankruptcy except for contributions made in the 12 months prior to bankruptcy. So if you make monthly contributions of $100 to your RRSP, the last $1,200 you contributed prior to bankruptcy will not be exempt. But everything else would be safe. (When I wrote this, the specific regulations governing the latest bankruptcy rules had not been published. Watch for more details as they become available.) Your CPP and OAS are also safe. So is your company pension plan.

Once you come out of bankruptcy, you must make saving a priority. While most people immediately focus on rebuilding their credit history, building assets is a great way to prove you've turned over a new leaf.

Your Employer Goes Bust

Your pension is most at risk if your company goes bust while your plan is underfunded. In the last market downturn, some defined benefit plans accumulated shortfalls because the plan's assets weren't big enough to cover the projected cost of future payouts. In December 2009, *MoneySense* magazine online said that, collectively, Canada's corporate pension plans were underfunded by $50 billion. Wow!

If you're scratching your head and wondering, "How can that be so? Don't they have to save that money?" you're in good company. In theory they have to save the money. But part of the formula for paying out a pension is based on the returns generated by the investments. No return, lower payouts.

While this is not a great place for your plan to be, as long as your employer remains solvent it may have no impact on you since there is time to make up the shortfall. If your pension plan divides the responsibility for a shortfall between you and you're employer, you'll both have to kick in more cash to make up the difference if markets don't recover. Or you'll have to settle for less income come pension time.

Since the law protects pensions that have already been earned, if you're already retired, a shortfall probably should not affect you, although there have been instances where retirees have had to bite the bullet and deal with a reduced pension benefit. The employee share of any shortfall becomes the still-working employees problem. They will have to contribute more money or agree to reduced benefits.

The worst case comes if your pension plan has a shortfall and your employer goes bust. Your pension might be reduced, but only by the extent of the shortfall, so you might lose something but you won't lose everything. Since pension assets are held in trust, a failing company can't use them to pay other creditors.

Most provinces have legislation to protect pensions. Ontario, for instance, has a Pension Benefits Guarantee Fund that's intended to cover pension underfunding up to certain limits if your employer bites the dust. But these funds are limited, and have been stressed of late, and there may not be enough money to cover potential shortfalls.

If you're scratching your head again and wondering what to do now, I don't have any easy answers for you. For some reason, we've deluded ourselves into thinking that the investment world has no risk. And just because your money is in a pension plan, that does not negate the risk it faces in the investment world. Life sometimes sucks.

SO LONG, FAREWELL

If you are in the asset-building stage of your life, you now have the tools you need to make some decisions about getting to the next stage of your life—retirement—with some money. You're probably feeling a whole lot less confused. Good. And you're ready to take the steps to start saving for the future, and start investing to make your money work hard. All that's left is for you to execute.

I can tell you what you need to know. I can show you how to make decisions. I can help you figure out what road you want to be on. But I can't do it for you. Only you can take the steps to get from where you are now to where you want to be. If you've just read the book and you're going to shelve it and do nothing, I'm sorry you wasted your money. But if you're going to act, this book was a good investment, and I'm very happy to have been able to help.

Don't be too quick to give this book away. The final part deals with what you need to think about as you move into retirement. It may be a dozen years before you need to look at Part 4: Pull the Chute. But I'll be here, between these covers, waiting for when you're ready.

Until then, remember, your life is yours to make of it what you will. And it's never too late to get started making it what you want it to be.

PART
FOUR

**PULL THE
CHUTE**

11

DECIDE IF YOU'RE READY

Retirement is so close you can taste it. For some the flavour is sweet like honey. You've done the preparation. You've set aside some money. You're feeling pretty good about what you've accomplished so far in your life. And you're not done yet.

For others, the approaching life-marker brings some trepidation. You don't know if you saved enough. You don't know what you'll do with yourself. You just don't know.

Whether you're feeling pretty sure of yourself or the thought of retirement has been keeping you up at night, this is the stage at which it makes sense to stop and take stock.

If you've been deluding yourself so far, it's time to wake up and smell the coffee. If you've been planning like a pessimist so you can live like an optimist, it's time to measure what you've accomplished so you can look forward eagerly and with passion.

The big question, really, at this stage of life is: When can I retire? And it's a question that only you can answer. To be confident in your decision, you should answer these three questions:

1. Do I have enough?
2. Have I had enough?
3. Do I have enough to do?

DO I HAVE ENOUGH?

We've been around this puppy a few times now, but ultimately this, and your health, will be the biggest determining factors. You need enough money to live—to meet all your needs. Then you may want some more money to support a lifestyle you'd like to live: your wants. Having enough money is a wholly personal thing; there's no magic number. You have to decide if what you have is enough.

You'll do this by taking stock of how much money you'll have to live on, and what you'll have to spend that money on: your income and your expenses. This is no time to be guesstimating. With retirement just around the corner, now is the time to nail down the numbers so that if there's a shortfall, you have some options in terms of filling the gap.

Your retirement income may come from these sources:

1. Government retirement benefits: OAS, CPP/QPP, GIS, and the like.
2. Company pension plan: defined contribution or benefit plan, group RRSP.
3. Registered retirement savings: an RRSP or RRIF, LIF, or LRIF.

4. Non-registered savings: your TFSA, other savings, investment portfolio, home equity, other personal property,
insurance cash value . . . almost anything you have that can
be turned into money.

On page 282 is a Retirement Income Worksheet that you
can use to make note of what you'll be getting from various
sources so you can total them up at the end. Grab your pen
and your calculator; it's time to face the music.

OAS

In 1952, Canada introduced the Old Age Security (OAS) system to provide income security universally across Canada.
The OAS system consists of

- OAS pension,
- Guaranteed Income Supplement (GIS), and
- Spouse's Allowance (SA).

OAS pension is a basic benefit paid monthly to all Canadians who are 65 or older and meet the Canadian residency
requirements. At the beginning of 2010, the maximum OAS
paid was $516.96 a month.

Not everyone gets the maximum. Service Canada's website
suggests that you think of OAS as a pie that's been divided
into 40 equal portions. To get the full pension, you have to
qualify for all 40 pieces. Less than 40 pieces? You'll get some
pension.

If you have been a resident of Canada for 40 years from

your 18th birthday, you'll get the max and you can skip on down to Applying for OAS.

If you haven't been a resident of Canada for 40 years after the age of 18, the number of pieces of pie you get depends on how many years you've lived in Canada after the age of 18. If you've been a resident for 36 years, you'll get 36 pieces of the pie, so you'll get 90% of the maximum.

$$36 \div 40 \times 100 = 90$$

If you've been a resident for 20 years, you'll get 20 pieces of the pie, or half the maximum.

$$20 \div 40 \times 100 = 50$$

From here the formula gets really complicated. If you were born before 1952, these special rules apply:

- you must have lived in Canada in 1977, or had a residence in Canada for some period,
- you must have had a valid immigration visa, AND
- you must have lived in Canada for the 10 years prior to your OAS approval, unless you didn't (see what I mean about complicated), in which case
  → You must have lived in Canada for the entire year before your approval AND
  → You must have lived in Canada since the age of 18 for three years for every year you were away during these last 10 years. Oy! My brain hurts!

If you don't meet the 40-year rule or qualify under the provisions for people born before 1952, you'll only get some of the 40 pieces of pie and only some of the OAS pension.

I immigrated to Canada in 1977 when I was 17. Man, did I just squeeze through the door or what? Since I will have lived here for 47 years by the time I turn 65, I'll get the full OAS. But what about my mother? She came to Canada when she was 37, so she'll only have lived here for 28 years, meaning she'll only get 28 of the 40 pieces of pie.

If 40 pieces of pie equal $516.96 a month, then 28 pieces of pie means she would get just ($516.96 ÷ 40 × 28 =) $361.87.

But wait. Since my Mom was born before 1952 and meets all the other criteria, she's in the clear and will get her full OAS after all.

 GAIL'S TIPS

. . . .

If you are an immigrant to Canada, you can't assume you're going to get the maximum OAS. You must call and find out specifically how much you will qualify for. This is especially true if you are banking on government benefits to meet most or all of your retirement income needs.

. . . .

Applying for OAS

OAS benefits aren't automatic; you have to apply for them. Apply six months before you turn 65 to ensure you begin receiving benefits on time. You can download an application kit or contact Service Canada to request that a kit be mailed to you.

Remember, too, that OAS benefits are taxable. Rate increases are calculated four times a year (January, April, July, and October) using the All-items Index from the Consumer Price Index (CPI) so that benefits keep up with the cost of living.

The OAS Clawback

Some time ago the government decided that our universal pension should not be quite so "universal" and began to means-test the OAS pension. If you make over a certain amount, you start to lose OAS benefits. For 2009, if you earned over $66,335, you had to give back 15 cents of OAS for every $1 of income above this limit. If you earned $107,692 or more, you lost the whole thing. The money is taken right off your OAS and is calculated based on your previous year's tax return.

So if you had an income of $75,000, you would lose (75,000 − 66,335 × 0.15 =) $1,299.75 of your annual OAS, or $108.31 a month.

Find out what you'll be entitled to from OAS and write it on your Retirement Income Worksheet on page 282.

The GIS

The Guaranteed Income Supplement is a monthly benefit paid to people who get an OAS pension but have little or no other income. It is based on your annual income combined with that of your spouse or common-law partner. Since income changes annually, you must apply for benefits every year, though you can reapply simply by filing your income tax return.

At the beginning of 2010, the maximum GIS benefit paid to an individual was $652.51 a month, and it was paid to individuals with an annual income of $15,672 or less. The spouse of a pensioner or someone also receiving the Spouse's Allowance receives less GIS. Benefits are not taxable. Service Canada has application forms.

If OAS is likely to be your only form of income, or your OAS and CPP combined will be less than $15,672, then you should add the GIS to your Retirement Income Worksheet.

Spouse's Allowance

The Spouse's Allowance (SA) is provided to partners of people who are receiving OAS. If you are between 60 and 64, and your family income does not exceed $28,992 (for 2010), you'll receive $947.86 a month. Normally, when the Feds' records show that you may be eligible for the SA, they send you an application kit. If you haven't received an application, but you think you may be eligible, contact Service Canada.

CPP/QPP

The Canada Pension Plan (CPP) and Quebec Pension Plan (QPP) are contributory plans, and benefits are based on earnings. The maximum monthly income available at the beginning of 2010 was $934.17. The exact amount you'll get depends on how much and for how long you contributed, and it's reported on your Statement of Contributions, which you can view online. Go to Service Canada and have a look at what you're likely to receive.

Before 1984, people had to wait until they turned 65 to be eligible to receive CPP/QPP benefits. Now you can get benefits as early as age 60 if you are considered to "have substantially ceased pensionable employment," which means your employment income isn't greater than the pension payable for that year.

Once upon a time, benefits were reduced 0.5% per month, or 6% per year, for every year before your 65th birthday. If you delayed taking benefits until after you turned 65 (the latest you can wait is till age 70), your benefits would be increased by 0.5% per month.

The 2009 federal budget proposed changes yet to be enacted at the time of writing. None of the proposed changes will affect anyone currently receiving CPP retirement benefits, or anyone who applies prior to the proposed changes taking effect. Here's what may change:

1. You won't have to stop working to collect your CPP, although collecting CPP while you're working means you're more likely to have your CPP grabbed back in taxes.

2. Currently, if you retire at 65 you can drop out seven of your lowest earning years from age 18 to 65. This lets you remove your lowest-income years when you may have been in school, were unemployed, or stayed home with your kids. The drop-out period is slated to go up to 7.5 years in 2012 and eight years in 2014.

3. If you collect CPP and then go back to work, you'll have to start making CPP contributions again if you're under 65. This is weird because you could potentially be collecting CPP and paying into CPP at the same time. Me'thinks this one wasn't really thought through very clearly. Or maybe it's simply a tax-grab.

4. If you take your CPP early, you'll lose more of your benefits since the calculation will go from 0.5% per month to 0.6% per month. So starting at age 60 would mean you'd lose 36% of your CPP instead of 30%. Clearly the government doesn't want you to take your CPP early.

5. On the flip side, though, they'll give you more if you delay taking your CPP. Instead of increasing benefits by 0.5%, you'll see an increase of 0.7% for every month you wait past your 65th birthday. So if you wait until you're 70, your benefits will go up by 42%, which can really help with inflation protection.

Decide When to Take CPP

So should you take CPP early or should you wait? The bird-in-the-hand camp does all kinds of calculations to show why you should not delay taking your CPP. They want to make sure you get your money back out of CPP before you croak since the death benefit paid is absolutely pathetic. You may have paid into CPP your whole life only to find that if you die early, all your estate will receive is six months' worth of your calculated retirement pension to a maximum of $2,500, not even enough to plant you in the ground. If you have a surviving life partner, that person will receive 60% of your benefits if he or she isn't currently receiving benefits. There is a downward sliding scale if your surviving partner is less than 65 years old, but to give you an idea of what CPP pays out, the average survivor's pension in 2002–2003 was just $280 a month.

The obvious answer to the question of when to start receiving CPP is whenever suits you more over the long run, not only taking into account how long you'll live and how much you'll get in the long haul, but your taxes as well. It also depends on whether you intend to spend the money or invest it for the future.

Generally, you'll benefit from taking benefits early if you're single, plan to spend the money, and are unlikely to live past 77. If you're married but your spouse won't receive the survivor benefits because they'll already receive the maximum CPP (or they'll predecease you), you'll also likely be better off drawing your benefits early. Of course, if you need the money immediately to meet your day-to-day living expenses, then go ahead and take your benefits early.

Consider waiting to take your benefits if your surviving spouse will need the survivor benefits from your plan to meet his or her needs. Also, if you expect to live a long, long time, or are concerned about the impact inflation will have on your income, waiting until age 65 or even 70 may be better for you.

 GAIL'S TIPS

If you plan to retire early, but intend to wait before claiming your CPP benefits, call and find out what the impact will be on your payments. Several years of no contributions before you've reached 65 may reduce the amount of pension to which you're entitled.

• •

Now that you know how much you'll be getting from CPP, plug your numbers into your Retirement Income Worksheet.

Figure Out Your Company Pension

If you're not going to get money from a company pension plan, you can skip ahead to "Calculate Your Expenses." If you have a pension plan at work, it's time to find out how much you'll likely receive.

Corporate pension plans fall into three basic categories:

1. **Defined benefit plans** (DBPs) incorporate a promise to pay out a regular income calculated according to a predetermined formula. With this type of plan, you'll know exactly how much you'll receive at retirement.
2. **Defined contribution plans** (DCPs), also referred to as money purchase plans, define the annual contributions required by the employer (and in many cases by the employee). How much you get out depends on the amount of money accumulated through contributions and earnings in the plan.
3. **Group RRSPs** function just like regular RRSPs except that they're created by an employer who often matches contributions up to a specific amount each year. The amount you get from a group RRSP, like a DCP, depends on how much you've accumulated.

The only way to know what your company pension plan will pay is to go and ask your benefits administrator. Get a statement showing how much your monthly benefit will be so you have something concrete to work with. Fill in that number on your Retirement Income Worksheet.

 GAIL'S TIPS

A pension buy-back is when you purchase additional credited service under an existing pension plan. More credited service means a higher pension. It may also mean you are able to retire earlier.

You may decide to do a buy-back to cover a maternity and parental leave if you did not contribute to your pension plan during your leave. Ditto if you've taken an authorized leave of absence without pay or if you ended up working a reduced workload for a period of time.

Since DBPs are based on your years of credited service in the pension plan, if you choose to buy back, you can

- increase your monthly pension benefit,
- retire with a full pension at an earlier date, and
- provide a larger survivor benefit for your spouse and/or your beneficiary after your death.

You can often pay for buy-backs in cash or through a payroll deduction. Retiring allowances can also sometimes be used for buy-backs.

• •

Know What Happens When You Die

Make sure that both you and your spouse have a good understanding of your pension benefits. It'll be important to know if your plan will continue to pay your spouse an income after you die.

Some company pensions end with the death of the pensioner. Others pay a reduced percentage to the surviving spouse. Some make a payout to your estate so your pension doesn't just evaporate.

If there is no continuation of income, or if that income will be reduced significantly, both you and your spouse will have to make some decisions about how you structure your other sources of retirement income. You may decide, for example, to hold onto your registered assets or unregistered investments to provide an income to the surviving spouse. Or you may continue paying the premiums on life insurance to provide the surviving spouse with future income.

Find Out If Your Pension Is Indexed

While you're in chatting with your benefits administrator, find out if your pension provides for full or partial indexing and when that indexing kicks in. Indexing is done to help a pension keep pace with inflation. When a pension is not indexed, over time the buying power of that pension income decreases.

Also check to see if your company plan is integrated. In other words, will your company benefits be blended with CPP to provide your income? If your company pension plan is integrated, whenever you get pension income estimates from your employer, don't double-count your CPP benefits.

Figure Out How Early Retirement Affects Your Pension

If early retirement is encouraged or available at your company, how will it affect your short-term (up to age 65) and long-term (after age 65) income? If your plan is integrated, will the company pay the CPP portion until you apply for benefits? Will your company increase your pension benefits to cover the amount you would have received if you had waited until 65 to claim your CPP benefits?

Now that you've learned what you need to know about your pension plan at work, input any changes to numbers in the worksheet.

CALCULATE YOUR EXPENSES

Okay, now that you know how much you're going to get from your government and/or company pension(s), it's time to figure out what your expenses will be. Only then can you know how big the gap is and how much you'll need from your savings to fill it.

Keep in mind that the costs you have early in your retirement are likely to change as you move through retirement. When you're 97, you may not be zipping around in your convertible anymore. And you may also need fewer new threads. But you can bet your first-born that your medical costs will go up.

• •

If you're pulling up to the retirement table, consider the extra spending you should do before you
move into living on a fixed, and potentially smaller,
income.

- Pay off your debts.
- Do major renovations, home repairs, and car repairs.
- Complete and pay off major purchases (like that RV or the new car).
- Have elective surgery using your accumulated sick leave.
- Have dental work completed.
- Get your eyes checked, and if you have a stable prescription, get an extra set of glasses.

• •

To figure all of this out, your next step is to create a budget
for your retirement's early days. You'll have to adjust your budget as you age and your needs change, just as you did before
you retired. Remember, a budget isn't cast in stone. It needs to
evolve as your life evolves.

Time to Make a Budget

If you're not living on a budget now, pulling numbers out of
the air won't do you a bit of good. Sure you can make the budget balance, but you won't be able to live on it. The only way to

know how much you'll spend during retirement is to start by knowing exactly how much you're spending now.

If you've never made a budget before, look back to pages 106 to 114, where I describe the process.

Once you've figured out what you're spending now, the next step is to identify how your expenses will change during retirement.

Grab four different-coloured highlighters and your budget. Highlight in different colours the expenses that will

- stay the same,
- go away,
- go down, and
- go up.

Which Expenses Will Stay the Same?

Some things never change . . . well, not on the day you retire. If you own your home, your house taxes and home insurance won't change. Neither will your car payments if you're still making them, or your mortgage payment if you're still making it. Ditto your utilities, your car insurance, and your auto-maintenance costs.

Go over you budget and highlight all the things that will likely stay the same. You always have the option of coming back to these numbers later, so it doesn't have to be perfect the first time.

Which Expenses Will Go Away?

If you plan to have your mortgage paid off—and you're within striking distance—this can save you big bucks when you move from a salary to living on a pension and your savings. And if your dependents have all struck out on their own, hey, that can save you big bucks too.

What else will go away? Maybe your car payment, if you planned it right. How about the money you were spending on parking? Lunches at work? Professional memberships and dues?

You're not saving for retirement anymore. And, hopefully, you already have a big fat emergency fund. You can eliminate savings from your budget.

You've paid off your debt too, right? Right? RIGHT?

Which Expenses Will Go Down?

With some planning and a little luck your taxes will be lower.

You're not driving to work every day, so you'll save money on gas. You might also save on car insurance, so get some fresh quotes.

You may feel that you have enough clothes so you can trim your clothing budget, particularly if you were buying clothes specifically for work.

Look at your life insurance coverage. If your mortgage is paid off, and your kids are out on their own, do you need as much insurance as you were carrying in your 40s? Don't just cancel it all. You'll have to do another needs assessment, especially if your partner will receive less income when you kick the bucket.

If you've been paying to have your house cleaned, your grass cut, or your home repairs done for you because you just didn't have time, these expenses may go away if you're happy to do them yourself.

If you were eating out a lot because you didn't have time to cook at home, your food costs may go down as you choose to do more in your own kitchen. Or they may go up if you decide that now that you don't have to cook for a family, you're content to eat all your meals down at Rosie's Diner.

Which of Your Expenses Will Go Up?

Medical needs will increase. Prescriptions are expensive. So is all the dental work you'll need done if your teeth start falling out. And then there's your fading eyesight. You better have some money built into your budget to buy all the masking tape and elastic bands it'll take to hold you together.

 GAIL'S TIPS

• •

On average, Canadians spend about $1,867 a year on health care, with the average senior couple coming in at about $2,738. You can use that as a rule of thumb when estimating how much to stick in your budget.

• •

Are you planning to travel more now that you have the time? How about that new hobby you've always wanted to take up, does it come with costs? Dinner out with friends twice a week? All that socializing and fun comes with a price tag.

Time to Plug In Numbers

Once you've determined which expenses will rise and which will fall, you're going to have to do some guessing about the actual numbers you will use in your budget. Since you are guesstimating these numbers, I strongly recommend that you add between 15% and 20% to each number you're changing, erring on the side of spending more. If you end up spending less, you'll have extra money to put towards your cruise. But if you underestimate your expenses, you'll be sorry.

If you have been spending $800 a month on food—whether that's eating in or eating out—and you think you'll only spend $600 once you retire, calculate your "cushion" like this:

$$\$600 \div 100 \times 15 = \$90$$

So you would put $690 in your budget.

Hey, wait a minute. Why am I bothering to do this if I'm going to end up with almost the same numbers?

I'll tell you why. We have a tendency to underestimate our expenses. No, I don't have any empirical proof of this, just years and years of experience working with hundreds and hundreds of people. When we underestimate, we set ourselves up to fail. Nobody ever got depressed because they had money left over. But not having enough money can make you very sad. So if you're going to guesstimate, you have to build in a safety zone so you don't end up sad and broke. Or you can do it your way, but then don't whine when you're short of money and miserable about having to tighten your belt.

FIGURE OUT THE GAP

Now that you know how much you'll be getting from your pension(s), and what your expenses are likely to be in retirement, you can calculate how much you'll need from your personal savings—registered and unregistered—to fill the gap.

1. Add up your income.

2. Add up your expenses.

3. Subtract your expenses from your income.

If you have a positive number at the bottom—congrats! It means you can live on your pension(s), and your savings are all available to play.

If you have a negative number at the bottom, you'll need to use your savings to fill the gap.

Figure Out What Your Savings Will Produce in Income

You don't have to close out your RRSP until the end of the year in which you turn 71, and many people choose to keep their registered assets in their RRSP (as opposed to using the money to buy an RRIF or annuity), taking what they need as cash withdrawals.

So how do you know how much of your money you will need to take from your savings to fill the gap between your pension income and your expenses?

Let's say your budget looks like this so far:

Government pension(s) $1,451
Plus private pension(s) $2,432

Total income (so far)	$3,883
Less Expenses	$4,615
Gap	-$732

Okay, you have to find $732 a month to cover your retirement expenses.

Figure Out Your Shortfall

Now let's say you have $125,000 in various RRSP and unregistered investments, on which you're earning an average return of 5%.

$$125,000 \times 5 = 625,000$$
$$625,000 \div 100 = 6,250$$

Annually, your savings are generating $6,250 in return, or $521 a month.

You've figured out your monthly gap is	$732
Your monthly return is $(6,250 \div 12)$	$521
Your monthly shortfall is $(732 - 521)$	$211

So you have to find an additional $211 a month, or $2,532 a year to meet your current retirement expenses.

Your registered and unregistered assets are made up of two parts: the income generated by your investments and the capital invested. While many people would like to be able to live on their income, never touching their capital, this often doesn't work in practise. You have to have a crap-load of money to get by using only the returns your investments generate, particularly if you have a conservatively invested portfolio and aren't earning a very high return. Even in times of higher interest rates, if inflation is also gobbling up your dollars they won't go as far, so you'll need more of them.

Regardless of whether you convert your RRSP to an RRIF or not (we'll cover this in greater detail later), figuring out how much your registered and unregistered assets are generating in income each year will let you know how much you're going to pull down on the principal each year.

If you were determined not to touch your principal, you could find some other way of generating that additional $211 a month: rent space in your home, take a part-time job, whatever you could come up with.

Using Your Principal

For now, let's assume you're not totally averse to touching your principal. In the case of this example, you'll have to take out a minimum of $211 from your principal monthly, or $2,532 a year, to make ends meet.

Time to learn about the 4% Rule, which can help you estimate the amount of money you can safely withdraw each year over a 25-year retirement. According to the 4% Rule, if you have a $200,000 portfolio and were retiring today, you could safely withdraw (200,000 ÷ 100 × 4 =) $8,000 in year one. You could then increase that amount every year with inflation and there's a 90% probability that you won't outlive your money.

Of course, if you want to be more conservative in your

investments and your estimates, you might change the 4% to 3.5%. And if you think you'll live longer than 25 years in retirement, you might want to run the numbers using 3%.

Alternatively, you can seek help from a financial advisor who has access to a calculator that can demonstrate how long your money will last.

 GAIL'S TIPS

Seeking help from a knowledgeable and reliable retirement-planning specialist may be a good idea at this point. Just make sure that you're not convinced to use assumptions you're not comfortable with, or talked in to making investments because your Spurt has scared your pants off. You're just fact-finding. You're gathering information. You're going to go home and process that information before you take any action. And if you walk away from the meeting a little shaky, pretty much convinced you're screwed, you'll want to get back to that computer and do your own research before you panic.

There are also some calculators on the web. While many of these are American, and I like to use Canadian calculators, this is one area where the calculator's place of origin has little impact, as long as there's no tax component to the calculation.

Gail Warning! It is with mixed feelings that I send you off to the web and the calculators available. When I was researching what's out there, I was astounded that I could put my figures into one calculator and hear that I'd be fine, and then put my figures into another calculator to learn that I'd be missing the mark. Exactly the same figures brought up different responses. This is the thing that ticks me off the most about the whole retirement-planning arena: It is as if some websites, some advisors, some tools want to doom you to failure in order to scare you into saving more money or into choosing investments with potentially higher returns.

In essence, what these calculators do is ask you:

- how much money you have (if you're only looking at your registered assets, only use this amount for this calculation).
- how many years your savings must last. (Yes, you're guessing. Have a look at how long your relatives lived when you guesstimate.)
- your return (if you're using a U.S. calculator, look for one that asks for "after-tax" return to keep the calculation straightforward).
- the inflation rate (yes, you're guessing again, but if you go with 2.5% to 3%, you shouldn't be too far off-base on historical figures).

The calculator will then tell you how much you can spend annually without your money running out.

Let's say you have $200,000, that you are 65, and that you want your money to last 20 years. You expect your after-tax return to be 5% and inflation to be about 2.5%. You'll be able to spend $12,452 every year and have the money last right up until you're 85.

The flaw in this system is that you'll get that same $12,452 every year, and you'll have to make it last even when inflation has reduced the buying power of your dollar.

Head back to your Retirement Income Worksheet and put in the amount you plan to spend from your principal every year.

STILL NOT ENOUGH?

You've figured out your income. You've calculated your expenses. You've filled the gap and closed the spread and you're still short of money. Now you have to get creative about how you'll make up the difference:

1. you can cut back on your expenses, or

2. you can make more money.

Sound familiar? It should. I've been singing this song for a long time now, and y'all should know the tune and the words by heart.

Step 1: Cut Back on Expenses

Time to go over your retirement expenses with a red pen, cutting back everything that isn't an absolute essential.

- How much money are you paying for auto insurance, electricity, heat, Internet, television, and phone? Are there ways that you can reduce your costs?

- Can you move to less expensive digs? Sure you like your home, but if it's eating up too much of your retirement dollars, it may be time to embrace change.

- Can you live without your car and all the attached expenses? Maybe you can if you move to a home within an easy walk to everything you need to live.

- Do you love to shop? If you're buying a lot of unnecessary things for the thrill of the shop, you could be dooming yourself to a very unhappy retirement because you won't squash your shopping bug. Start using a list to get the impulse monkey off your back. If you see something you like, add it to your list. If you have the money you can go back and buy it. If you don't, oh well.

- Are you taking advantage of seniors' discounts? Loads of businesses, including your bank, many restaurants, and some retail stores let you buy at a discount if you follow their rules. If you know you qualify for a senior discount, ask for it. Don't wait for it to be offered.

- Are you doing too many expensive activities? Some hobbies and activities are cheap. Some are expensive. If you love to knit, that can be an inexpensive pastime if you just buy as much wool as you need for each project. But if you turn knitting into an excuse for shopping, filling drawer upon drawer with wool, buying every knitting magazine that exists, then you've taken knitting into another realm. Ditto if you love to golf but can't be satisfied with a once-a-week game. Can you do less of the stuff that eats money, and more of the stuff that doesn't, like volunteering?

- Are you eating out a lot? When my grandparents retired, they went to lunch in the same restaurant every day. It was a way of getting out of the house and a way of socializing a little. They always had the special, whatever the special was, and that put some variety into their meals. I think my grand-mother had had enough of cooking. If you can afford to do this, hey, have a nice lunch. But if your eating out is throwing your budget out of whack, you may have to limit your out-ings. Substitute potluck dinners with friends. You'll still get the variety and the socializing but it'll cost a lot less money.

- Are you bailing out your kids or grandkids? It's all well and good to want to help, and if you have loads of money and it won't affect your life, then maybe you can. But if you're going to give up some of your own needs and wants because your children won't stand on their own two feet, you're a dope. Yes, some children do find themselves in desperate times. And our hearts ache for them. And we want to help. But if you're always bailing out some fool who doesn't have the good sense God gave a goose, you're not actually helping. You're just delaying the inevitable. Stop.

There are about 1,000 ways to save money: from buying pre-owned to paying bills online so you save on postage, to cancelling magazine subscriptions and getting a library card. Go through your budget with a fine-tooth comb.

If you hate the idea of cutting back, or if you've done it and there still isn't enough to get to the end of the month before you get to the end of the money, go to Step 2.

Step 2: Make More Money

There are loads of ways to supplement your income, particularly if you are healthy and you are in the early stages of retirement. You could try one or more of these ideas:

- Take a part-time job. Many retailers need part-time employees and some only want you to work 10 to 15 hours a week. This may be the perfect way to make your grocery, travel, or entertainment money.

- Start a new business. Whether you use your existing skills or learn new skills to start your own business, this is one of the most creative ways of making more money. If you were an accountant or bookkeeper, offer your services to small businesses that may not be able to afford full-time staff. Your sewing skills could be brought to focus on designing clothing or doing alterations. You could become a computer consultant, a web designer, or a freelance writer.

- Generate income from your hobby. Can you teach knitting at a local wool store or community centre? How about teaching piano or guitar a couple of evenings a week? It'll be something to do and you'll make a couple of bucks to boot.

- Find a roommate. If you have a spare bedroom, a roommate may not only mean help with the rent or maintenance and utilities, but company too. Ask friends if they know of someone looking for a place to live. Place ads on community bulletin boards and in local newspapers with a clear description of your space, the cost, and the specifics of the roommate you're looking for. Alternatively, you can take in students and charge room and board if you want to make it a seasonal thing.

- Convert part of your home to a rental. This moves the roommate a few steps away from your personal space, and takes some planning, and likely some money, since if you don't already have an "apartment" you'll have to create one.

- Sell your home and downsize. Even if your home is paid off, your maintenance costs, taxes, and utilities may be more than you can manage. Consider relocating to a more affordable home. If you decide to rent, the money from the sale of your home can do wonders to supplement your retirement savings.

LAST CHANCE

It's your last chance to make some changes before you hit the retirement road. Have you considered all your options? Really considered them? Remember, you have control over what you do with your money now and when you're retired. But you have to decide what's really important to you and then take the steps to prioritize those important things over the every-day not-so-important things that can grab your attention and satisfy your consumerism itch.

Are you going to rein in your spending and use the money you've cut from your expenses to boost your savings? Have you gone over your current expenses and eliminated little costs here and there? You'll be surprised at the difference it may make. And if you're close to retirement, practising to live on less now will stand you in good stead when you're living on your retirement income.

Have you seriously considered how to boost your earnings? Can you take a second job? Are there ways to increase the money currently coming in? Look around for ways to make a little extra money. This goes hand in hand with . . .

Delaying your retirement. The later you retire, the more time you have to save and the more time your money has to grow before you have to start pulling on it.

You can also plan to work during retirement; you'll stretch your retirement savings even further. Do you have an inter-est or hobby you could turn into a money maker? Would you consider working part-time in a completely new field? Be cre-ative. Don't underestimate the value of your skills.

And there's always the equity in your home. Whether you decide to downsize, sell and rent, or use a reverse mortgage (not my favourite), your home equity may be a good source of additional retirement income.

Finally, remember that your retirement savings are made

up of both income earned on your savings and also your principal. Does this sound obvious? A lot of people resist drawing on their principal during retirement for fear that they will outlive their money. If necessary, take your figures to a financial advisor who can show you exactly how long your principal will last. And for those of you hell-bent on leaving an estate for your children, that only makes sense if you can do so comfortably. Living like a pauper so you can pass on your money to your kids is dumb! You did it on your own. Now it's their turn.

HAVE I HAD ENOUGH?

Some people can't wait to hang up their fiddles. If you've had enough, it may be time to move on to new things. For others, the idea of leaving their passion behind to do something else seems dumb. After all, if you're living your dream, why stop.

Perhaps the biggest clue that you've had enough is the fact that you're questioning whether it's time to quit. People who are happy doing what they're doing seldom question the need to continue working. Those who are not happy, who may feel obsolete, who are tired of "the grind," are the people who are most likely to ask, "Have I had enough?"

If you think of retirement as an end, you may be doing yourself a huge disservice. After all, you may spend almost as much time retired as you did working. But to know just how you feel, you should think about what's motivating you to retire.

1. Have you outgrown your career? Sometimes when you do the same thing for a long time you just get tired of it. Sure, you grew and developed new skills when you were excited about what you did. But you've outgrown the excitement and now it's just same-old, same-old. If the challenges are gone, you may think you're ready for retirement when, in fact, you're ready for new challenges.

2. Are you burnt out? If your job is stressful, if it carries a lot of emotional baggage, you could simply be exhausted. If you haven't taken the time to recharge your batteries physically, emotionally, and spiritually, you could be running on empty. Maybe it isn't retirement you need so much as a sabbatical. Or a complete change of scenery.

3. Have you been downsized? Can't imagine anyone else wanting you? Figure this is the end of the line? Turn your thinking around and you could be looking at a great opportunity to use your skills in new ways. Don't attempt to dive into the same job in a new location. Or worse, don't just throw up your arms in resignation. The universe is telling you there are new and different things to experience. Embrace the change. Choose to be excited about the opportunity. Breathe some life into that long-forgotten dream of yours.

4. Is your internal GPS telling you to change direction? You want more control over your time. You crave the freedom to do more of what you love and less of what you tolerate. Listen to your small voice. Follow your intuition. Start creating your exit strategy so that you can leave what must be left behind on your terms.

5. Are you feeling less well? Illness is a big reason people choose to retire. According to the 2007 General Social Survey done by Stats Canada, of those people who consider their health only fair to poor, over 23% plan to retire before age 60 and half expect that their income will not be sufficient. If you fall into the "sick and poor" category, you're going to have to reconcile yourself to a simple life and find ways to take joy from the small things. Spirituality may be very important in helping you to deal with this. So, too, will a strong network of family and friends, so don't plan on moving away from your pals. But do plan for ways to minimize your costs by doing things like sharing accommodation, volunteering for social interaction, or growing your own veggies in the summer.

DO I HAVE ENOUGH TO DO?

Don't underestimate the importance of this question. You're going to have to fill 168 hours a week. Sure, you'll do some sleeping—there's 42 hours you don't have to worry about—but what's your plan for the other 18 hours a day, Monday through Sunday, January through December, for the next 20, 25, or 30 years?

 GAIL'S TIPS

• •

Ever heard the term "leisure sickness"? It was coined by the Dutch psychologist Ad Vingerhoets of Tilburg University. He found that of the almost 2,000 people in a study, about 3% got sick when they didn't have enough to do. Turns out some people don't like to relax, and their bodies punish them if they try. For years they ignored the twinges that signalled the onset of illness and overdosed on the adrenaline their ultra-busy lives created. (Adrenaline is an immune system booster.) But with not enough to do, they become super-sensitive to these twinges, and with not enough adrenaline they become ill, some quite seriously.

If you think you might suffer from leisure sickness, make sure you build enough meaningful activity into your day-to-day life. And get some exercise; it's great for reducing negative stress. Put some effort in to developing a better sense of life-work balance.

• •

The number one thing on most people's minds is the financial impact of the end of the paycheque.

The second significant change you'll face, and the one most people don't think about enough, is the psychological impact of leaving work. This will differ from person to person depending on how much the job has functioned as a source of identity, provided social contacts, and served to structure time. The more dependent you have been on your work for your friendships and your fun, the more careful you must be about planning how to cope with The Change.

How often have you been asked (or asked of someone else), "What do you do?" If your work functions as a source of status and self-esteem for you, retirement may mean a loss of identity and a feeling of less personal worth. If you put a great deal of emphasis on what you do for a living, you must take time to determine if it is only your work by which you define yourself, or if there are other aspects of your life that contribute to your status, identity, and self-esteem.

Often when people leave work, they have difficulty maintaining their work-based relationships. Part of your planning for retirement should focus on building a network of relationships that are not dependent on your work environment. You'll need to find ways to replace friendships that may disappear. Joining organizations, participating in activities in which you already have interests, and exploring new areas of interest before you leave work all help ease the transition.

Work provides a structure for the use of time. Many of us are conditioned to working full days, usually against time pressures. Before you actually retire, the thought of having unlimited time to do whatever you want may seem like Utopia. However, unless your time is structured and includes obligations requiring effort on your part, all that time can become boring and frustrating.

Some people find it difficult to use their time meaningfully once the formal structure of work disappears. It is not enough to fill your time by just keeping busy. You need to use your time in ways that will be personally satisfying. If you have skills from your work life that can be transferred to other activities, you may want to think about working part-time, consulting, starting your own business, or volunteering.

Figure Out Where Your Time Goes

Do you have a good handle on how you spend your time right now? Most of us don't. Here's how to get a snapshot of what your do with your time right now.

Create a chart that includes seven blocks, each divided into 24 pieces. That's your week, divided into hours. Make at least one extra copy.

Colour in the segments based on what you're doing with your time right now:

- Light blue for the hours you spend on work-related activities. If you bring work home or spend time commuting, include that time.
- Red for the hours you spend on personal care activities, such as showering, eating, and exercising.
- Yellow for the hours you spend sleeping.
- Purple for the hours you spend attending to your household duties: housekeeping, cooking, shopping, laundry, gardening, snow shovelling, and the like. If you spend time on occasional jobs, such as doing home repairs, include those.
- Green for the time you spend casual socializing with your family and friends.
- Orange for the time you spend in leisure activities: sports, hobbies, and activities involving others.
- Brown for the time you spend in solitary activities like reading, watching television, listening to music.
- Dark blue for the time you spend in formal socializing as a member of a club, organization, volunteer group, etc.

Next, colour in the second chart to show how you would like your time to look during retirement. Keep in mind that with reduced time spent on family maintenance (with the kids gone you'll have less laundry, less vacuuming, less cooking), work, professional associations, and other pre-retirement activities, you'll have to allocate more time to other activities.

Remember that many of your current interests will be important to you when you retire. If you are an avid gardener now, you will likely want to continue gardening. Look for a community centre that provides greenhouse facilities for the winter. Join a garden club. Or build a solarium on your home before you retire so that when you move into retirement, you've got a place to putter around.

Since retirement means leaving colleagues with whom you interacted eight or more hours a day, five days a week, you'll likely miss some of them. Or you may realize that the only thing you had in common with your colleagues was work. It will be important to cultivate friends outside of your workplace by getting involved in your community. Take up a new hobby. Join an association. Volunteer. Find places to make new friends.

Your partner will have something to say about the way you both spend your time. Work together so that no conflicts arise later. You might be surprised at just how different you both feel about what will happen during retirement. While the two of you should do this exercise individually, you must also come together and share your ideas so that you have mutually agreeable expectations.

You may end up spending part of your retirement alone. If you're a woman, this is most likely since women tend to live longer than men. Make sure you know your financial position. Also, make sure you develop an emotional support system of family, friends, and activities so that you do not feel alone and abandoned.

 GAIL'S TIPS

Do not make a major lifestyle decision in the first 12 months of retirement unless you planned to do so well before your retirement date and it is part of your retirement strategy. While you may be tempted to move house or move country, retirement is stressful enough. Perspective on everything changes once you do retire. Take your time. Your wants or needs will change and you should give them a chance to settle down so you can make good decisions about the rest of your life.

Your family may have strong opinions about what you should or should not do with your retirement. You may want to spend time in a warm place while your children want you to be readily available to them. You won't have to live your life for them (those days are gone), but you should try to be sensitive to their feelings. They may need reassurance about your financial, emotional, and health circumstances. They will also be facing their own demons as your retirement brings them face-to-face with the fact that they are also aging.

With time on your hands and money in the bank, you're ready to take the next step: deciding how to make best use of all those savings you've accumulated. And that's what we'll talk about in the next chapter.

Retirement Income Worksheet

Monthly Income	$
OAS	_____
GIS	_____
Spouse's Allowance	_____
CPP/QPP	_____
Company pension plan(s)	_____
Other pension	_____
Total Monthly Income	_____
Total Monthly Expenses (take this total from your Budget Worksheet on p.132)	_____
Monthly Income	_____
− Monthly Expenses	_____
= **Gap**	_____
Income from registered savings	_____
+ Income from non-registered savings	_____
= **Total Income from Savings**	_____
Gap	_____
− Total Income from Savings	_____
= **Gap to Fill**	_____

12

MAKE IT HAPPEN

Retirement time! You've planned. You've done the math. You've figured out what you want from the next chapter of your life. Now comes the part where you decide how to take out all that money you've saved in a way that minimizes your taxes and maximizes your spending power.

There are many different ways to move from saving mode to spending mode, and the legislators and the financial industry have done their level best to make sure that most ways are royally confusing. Let's see if I can help you to make some sense of it all. If you get lost, put the book down for a while, take a break, and come back. Just because the rules are complicated doesn't mean you can afford to ignore them.

TAXES

The only savings vehicle that has absolutely no tax liability is a TFSA. So any money you pull from your TFSA will have no taxes that you need to pay attached.

Your government pension—OAS or CPP—will be taxed. So, too, will your company pension plan. When you take money out of your RRSP or your RRIF, you will have to pay tax on that money. And even your unregistered assets will incur a tax liability on the return they earn or on their sale if you make a profit. Yes, taxes will be with you until you die.

 GAIL'S TIPS

• •

If your retirement income is considerably higher than your life partner's, you'll probably end up paying more tax than necessary. One way to deal with this problem is to split your CPP benefits with your spouse so they receive more income while you receive less. This can help to reduce the OAS clawback and potentially put you in a lower tax bracket so you'll lower your total family tax bill. (QPP benefits cannot be split.)

To split your CPP benefits with your spouse, you must both be 60 or older and apply for your CPP benefits at the same time. The amount you can split is the number of years you've been married, expressed as a percentage of the total years of CPP contributions. So if you have been married for 20 years and your buddy has contributed to CPP for 25 years, you can split up to 80% of your benefits (20 [years of marriage] ÷ 25 [years of contribution] x 100 = 80%). The total amount eligible for splitting will be divided equally between both partners.

• •

I could write an entire book on how your retirement income may be taxed and how to minimize those taxes. I'm not gonna. You should either get yourself a software program to calculate your taxes or see a professional who can guide you through the maze of tax rules, credits, and deductions. Suffice to say, for our purposes, you have to keep in mind that each of your sources of income comes with a tax liability, and you have to know what that expense is likely to be to adequately prepare for it.

CONVERT YOUR RRSPs

The most popular way for Canadians to convert their RRSP savings is using a Registered Retirement Income Fund or RRIF, which creates a flow of income during retirement. I like RRIFs because they provide the flexibility to design an income stream that meets your specific needs in terms of both amount and frequency. They also give you the ability to increase or decrease your income as your needs change.

Your money continues to be tax-sheltered as long as it remains in the RRIF, and you pay tax only on the money you take out each year. So, basically, an RRIF is a continuation of your RRSP, but instead of putting money in, you're taking money out. You can hold the same investments as you did in your RRSP and your money will continue to grow on a tax-deferred basis. This is not a small thing. Since you're likely to be retired for a long time—if you retire at 65 and live to 85, that's two decades of growth—you'll still have time to make compounding work for you.

You can open an RRIF at any age and roll over as much or as little of your RRSP dollars as you wish. However, you must do something with your RRSPs by the end of the year in which you turn 71. Many people hold off for as long as they can to maximize their tax-deferred compounding and then convert their RRSPs to an RRIF to continue the tax deferral for as long as they possibly can.

 GAIL'S TIPS

• •

If you're under the age of 71 and need to take an income from your retirement savings, you do not have to convert your RRSPs to an RRIF to do so, since you may make a withdrawal from an RRSP at any time. However, if you're planning to make a withdrawal from a Spousal RRSP and you don't want the money withdrawn taxed in the hands of the contributor, you should convert to an RRIF first, since the minimum withdrawal amount is taxed in the hands of the plan holder.

• •

KNOW HOW MUCH YOU MUST TAKE FROM A RRIF

There is a legislated minimum annual payout (MAP) that must be paid from the RRIF each year, except in the year the

RRIF is opened. For the year in which the RRIF is set up, the MAP is considered to be zero.

There are a bunch of complicated rules used to calculate the MAP. I don't know why the legislation is so obtuse!

- There are "qualifying" and "non-qualifying" RRIFs:
    → A "qualifying" RRIF was opened before 1993 and has not accepted new money since 1992 except from another qualifying RRIF. Since it's been almost 20 years, many RRIFs are now "non-qualifying."
    → A "non-qualifying" RRIF was opened after 1992 or received money from a plan opened after 1992.
- Your age also has an impact on whether the Age Formula or the Percentage Formula is used:

Age at January 1*	Type of RRIF	Calculation
Under 71	Any RRIF	Age Formula
71–78	Qualifying	Age Formula
71–78	Non-qualifying	Percentage Formula
79 or over	Any RRIF	Percentage Formula

*of the year you open the plan

The Age Formula

If you're under 71 when you convert your RRSP to an RRIF, the Age Formula is used. Ditto if your RRIF is "qualifying." Here's the formula:

Market value of the RRIF at Dec. 31 ÷ (90 − plan holder's age at Dec. 31)

Let's say your RRIF is worth $100,000 on December 31, and that you're 63 years old. The formula would look like this:

$$100,000 \div (90 - 63) = 3,704$$

So the minimum amount you'd have to take from the RRIF would be $3,704 for the year. Not much, eh? Well, that's because the calculation of the MAP is meant to let as much money stay inside the RRIF as possible so that it lasts you right up until your last breath. The Percentage Formula shows this quite clearly.

The Percentage Formula

If you're 71 and your RRIF is non-qualifying, or if you're 79 or over, then the Percentage Formula kicks in. Here's the formula:

% based on age × RRIF value on Jan. 1

You need this chart to make the Percentage Formula work:

Age on January 1	Qualifying RRIFs	Non-Qualifying RRIFs
69	4.76%	4.76%
70	5.00%	5.00%
71	5.26%	7.38%
72	5.56%	7.48%
73	5.88%	7.59%

Age on January 1	Qualifying RRIFs	Non-Qualifying RRIFs
74	6.25%	7.71%
75	6.67%	7.85%
76	7.14%	7.99%
77	7.69%	8.15%
78	8.33%	8.33%
79	8.53%	8.53%
80	8.75%	8.75%
81	8.99%	8.99%
82	9.27%	9.27%
83	9.58%	9.58%
84	9.93%	9.93%
85	10.33%	10.33%
86	10.79%	10.79%
87	11.33%	11.33%
88	11.96%	11.96%
89	12.71%	12.71%
90	13.62%	13.62%
91	14.73%	14.73%
92	16.12%	16.12%
93	17.92%	17.92%
94	20.00%	20.00%
95+	20.00%	20.00%

Let's say your RRIF is worth $100,000 on January 1 and that you're 71 years old. For a qualifying RRIF, the formula would look like this:

$$100{,}000 \times 5.26 \div 100 = \$5{,}260$$

So the minimum amount you'd have to take from the RRIF would be $5,260 for the year. You're probably dying with curiosity about how much more or less that would be if the Age Formula were used.

$$100{,}000 \div (90 - 71) = 5{,}263$$

We definitely needed to revamp the formula so that we wouldn't take that extra $3 a year out of our RRIFs too early. (Heavy note of sarcasm here!)

So why do we make things so complicated? Who the hell knows. It may be to keep The Legislators in business. It may be to give The Spurts something to talk about. In the end, it makes our lives more complicated for very little gain.

Thank heavens we're almost done with this qualifying and non-qualifying nonsense, although I'm sure we'll find a way to muck up the legislation some more to keep us guessing. But you can take heart in knowing that once you hit the age of 77, it's all the same anyway. For now, at least.

The important thing is not to let the legislation and the made-up complications scare you. Yes, it may take a while and some effort to figure this stuff out, but you shouldn't give up. After all, it's your money and you've worked very hard for it. And it's your life and you want it to be just so. Putting in a little effort to get over the humps—even if they are man-made and pretty ridiculous humps—will be worth it in the end.

WITHDRAWALS FROM A SPOUSAL PLAN

One of the areas most misunderstood when it comes to Spousal RRSPs are the rules regarding withdrawals. While only the plan holder may take money out of a Spousal RRSP, the tax owed can be attributed back to the contributor if you're not careful about when you take the money out.

The funds will be taxed in the plan holder's hands only if no contribution has been made to ANY Spousal RRSP in the year of withdrawal or the two preceding calendar years.

 GAIL'S TIPS

If you're going to take money from a Spousal RRSP and want to avoid having the income taxed in the hands of the contributor, then either

- stop all contributions to spousal plans three calendar years prior to the withdrawal, or
- convert the RRSP to an RRIF and take only the minimum annual payment, which will not be taxed as the contributor's income.

If a contribution of any kind has been made during the year of withdrawal or the two preceding calendar years, anything contributed and then withdrawn in that three-year window will be taxed in the contributor's hands.

Use of the term "calendar year" is significant. Since the rule applies to the year of the withdrawal plus the two preceding calendar years, the timing of the contribution to a Spousal RRSP is important. If, for example, you made a spousal contribution in December 2010 and no further contributions, the fund would be taxed in the plan holder's hands as early as January 2013. However, if you made the contribution in February 2011, the earliest you would be able to withdraw the funds without attribution would be January 2014.

 GAIL'S TIPS

• •

Because of the three-year calendar rule for contributions to a Spousal RRSP, it is better to make contributions by December 31 and not go into the 60-day grace period that follows.

• •

If someone tells you the spousal rule is based on anything other than "calendar" years, they're wrong. I'm appalled by the amount of incorrect information that exists on the websites of reputable companies. Apparently no one thinks it's important to delete old and outdated information. The good and the bad reside side-by-side, leaving consumers to try to figure out what's right and what's wrong. Always check the publication date of whatever it is you're reading, and if it seems old, verify using a more up-to-date source.

The rules that say the money will be taxed in the contributor's hands don't apply if

- the contributing spouse dies in the year of the withdrawal,
- you or your partner is a non-resident when the funds are withdrawn,
- you and your partner are living separate and apart at the time of withdrawal because of a relationship breakdown, or
- the Spousal RRSP funds are
  → transferred to another Spousal RRSP,
  → transferred to a Registered Retirement Income Fund (RRIF) and only the minimum amount is withdrawn, or
  → used to purchase a life annuity, term certain annuity to age 90, or registered pension plan, provided the plan can't be commuted for three years.

 GAIL'S TIPS

If you're over 71 and can no longer contribute to an RRSP, and if you're required to take money out of your RRIF but don't need the income to live on, you can use a TFSA to shelter at least a portion of what you have to take into income. Since TFSAs have no top-end age restrictions—they don't have to mature by a certain age—you can use them to shelter income for the future for emergencies or simply to help stave off the ravages of inflation.

MAINTAIN YOUR FLEXIBILITY

The main advantage of a RRIF is its flexibility. Unlike an annuity (which we'll talk about shortly), which is a set-in-stone decision, with a RRIF you can change your mind at almost any time, depending on the underlying investments you're holding. You can change your asset mix. You can take out more money than the minimum amount. And when you no longer want to be concerned with the management of your investments, you can buy an annuity using your RRIF assets.

 GAIL'S TIPS

• •

In Canada, the first $1,000 of pension income is earned tax-free. The pension income tax credit is what you claim on your tax return to get that $1,000 without having to pay any tax on it. If you have no other source of pension income (you need "pension income" specifically to claim the $1,000 pension income tax credit), then roll as much as you will need each year to a RRIF (it'll be the $1,000 plus the applicable withholding taxes if the $1,000 is above your minimum annual payout amount), and take the full amount as a lump-sum withdrawal so you can receive this money tax-free.

If you weren't all that up on income splitting and think you missed the boat, I have some good new for you. If you are 65 or older, you may be able to allocate up to 50% of any income that qualifies for the pension income tax credit to your life partner. If you're under 65 and your income comes from an annuity bought with money from a registered pension plan, you too may be able to pension-split. Check with your tax advisor to see if you can.

• •

LIFS/LRIFs

If you belonged to a company pension plan and left that employer, your company pension may have been transferred to a Locked-in Retirement Account (LIRA). When it comes time to take money out of the LIRA, you won't be able to do so using a regular RRIF. You'll have to use an LRIF (locked-in RIF) or a LIF (life income fund).

LIFs are available almost everywhere (PEI was the exception when I last checked), and LRIFs can be purchased in Ontario, Manitoba, Saskatchewan, and Newfoundland. Both operate much the same way: There's a minimum income you must take, and an optional maximum that may be applied. Once upon a time, conversion to an annuity was mandatory just about everywhere by age 90, but that's disappeared in all jurisdictions except New Brunswick, so most people may retain control over how their retirement assets are invested.

If you live in Saskatchewan or Manitoba, you have the option of choosing a Prescribed Retirement Income Fund (PRIF) that has a minimum withdrawal limit, but no maximum. Your spouse is automatically named as your beneficiary unless they sign a waiver letting you designate someone else.

● ●

If you're 55 or older, you can make a one-time conversion of up to 50% of a federally regulated LIF to an RRSP or RRIF, which eliminates the upper limit on how much you can take out each year. And if you have a small LIF balance, you can unlock these assets. As long as your LIF holdings are 50% or less of the yearly maximum pensionable earnings (YMPE), you can transfer the full amount to an RRSP or RRIF, or the LIF may be wound up and you can take the entire amount as cash.

FYI: The YMPE is calculated annually and is the maximum earnings for which contributions can be made to the Canada Pension Plan or Quebec Pension Plan during the year. For 2009, when the YMPE was set at $46,300, the limit was set at $23,150.

● ●

This is yet another example of too much legislation making the rules more complex than they need be. Federal and provincial governments keep messing around with the legislation creating more rules and more confusion. Yes, some people are morons and it would be nice to think we could protect fools from themselves. But we can't. And for the government—federal or provincial—to tell people how and when they can use their money is ridiculous. It would be far better if they spent their time making sure that when companies went belly-up, they didn't take people's hard-earned and "guaranteed" retirement plans with them.

If you have a Locked-in Retirement Account, figure out what the minimum amount of income you must take is and how much tax you'll pay. Then decide if you are going to pull the minimum, more than the minimum, or convert to an annuity to make this money work for you. In all likelihood, an advisor with some experience with this decision will be very useful at this point.

ANNUITIES

If you convert to a RRIF, you have to manage your own portfolio of investments. If you're sick and tired of thinking about money and all you want is a regular stream of income you don't have to worry about, then you may want to buy an annuity.

When you buy an annuity, you give an insurance company, bank, or trust company your money in exchange for a promise of a specific amount of income each month. The really big thing to know about an annuity is that the payout is based on where interest rates are when you purchase the annuity. During periods of high interest rates an annuity can really make your hard-earned money sing since you're locking in that high rate for the life of the plan. When rates are low, not so much. And while it may look like "the easy way out" when the option is presented to you, when interest rates do go up again, you'll be kicking yourself in the pants that you didn't have the guts, the foresight, the fortitude to hold out for a better return.

There are two basic types of life annuities:

1. A straight life annuity provides a regular income payout over your entire life. When you croak, it's gone.

2. A fixed-term annuity pays out a specific amount based on the term you've chosen, but for no longer. Guess right about how long you'll live and you'll have money right up until the end of your days. Guess wrong and you'll be old and poor. Not pretty. Terms range from 5 years to 20 years, and the amount you receive will go down the longer the term you have chosen. However, if you die before the end of the term, the remaining amount will be paid to the person you've named as your beneficiary, or to your estate.

Of course, just as you can get chocolate ice cream with marsh-mallows and almonds—yum, Rocky Road, my favourite—so, too, can you get annuities that have extra stuff in 'em.

You can buy a joint and last survivor annuity that provides income over your or your partner's life so your partner is covered, although there may be a drop-off in the amount they receive.

You can buy a life annuity that offers a guaranteed number of payments (usually from 5 to 20 years) so that there's money left over for your estate should you pop off early in the contract. Of course, the longer the guarantee, the less you'll receive monthly.

You can buy an annuity with an indexed option to help you keep pace with inflation. Or one that is accelerated if you can prove that you'll have a shortened life expectancy. Or one that is deferred where you give them your money now and it can grow but you don't take an income until a date in the future.

The amount you receive depends on several factors, including how much money you have, how long you're expected to live, your sex (because goils live longer than boys), and the interest rate in effect when you buy the annuity. Remember, low interest rates mean lower monthly incomes, which is one reason why annuities tend to decline in popularity when interest rates are in the dumper.

 GAIL'S TIPS

• •

Remember, if you buy an annuity with assets from an RRSP or RRIF, this is called a "registered annuity" and all the income received is taxable in the year you receive it. So don't forget to calculate the cost of the tax in when figuring out how much you'll actually have to live on.

Annuities can be purchased with cash—referred to as a prescribed annuity—and these annuities are taxed based on the interest to be earned over the life of the whole contract spread evenly over all the payments. This provides an element of tax deferral, except in the case of "accelerated annuities," which are based on a shortened life expectancy.

• •

The potential downside to an annuity is that you'll be living on a fixed income, since the monthly payments remain the same over the life of the annuity. What seems a princely sum at the outset may feel like a pauper's allowance in 20 years. Remember, too, that surviving spouses usually receive less income. The death of the first spouse often means about a 40% drop-off, so the survivor receives only about 60% of the original income amount.

That doesn't mean I'm completely down on annuities. I think they have a place for people who want a guaranteed income and don't want to have to think about managing their money. But you have to be careful not to buy 'em when rates are low and headed up or jump into them too early so that the payout is pathetic.

An annuity contract is cast in concrete; you can't change your mind. That's fine if interest rates are in the mid-teens (yes, I was there the last time this happened) and you don't want to have to think about your money any more. But it's not okay when rates are low and you've got your senses about you and can take responsibility for managing your own money. You can always move into an annuity, but you can't move out of one. So take care with your decision to choose this option.

 GAIL'S TIPS

. . . .

Annuities are another of those products that are surrounded by complicated language created to make you feel like a moron. Honestly! You'd think that after all these years we'd be more focused on simplicity and clarity than on bafflegab. Not so when it comes to annuities. Don't be pushed into something you don't understand. Get your annuity salesperson to explain it to you until you can explain it to your grandchild. Get lots of quotes when looking for the right product for you. You won't believe how different the payouts can be from one annuity provider to another. Do your homework. Know what you're buying. Get the very best deal you can.

REVERSE MORTGAGES

If you've got a ton of equity in your home and you're cash poor, you may be tempted to look at a reverse mortgage to get at some of that equity to make your cash flow a little richer. I'm not a big fan of reverse mortgages. I see them as a solution of last resort. But for those people who believe a reverse mortgage is just the ticket, here's what you need to know.

While there are different flavours of reverse mortgages, over 90% of all plans sold in Canada fall into the "simple reverse mortgage" category. A simple reverse mortgage is the opposite of the regular mortgage with which most of us are familiar. Instead of trying to build up equity through your mortgage payments, with a reverse mortgage you take equity out of your home. You're charged interest on the balance that has been advanced to you, and you have the choice of paying the interest annually or having the interest capitalized, which means it's added to your outstanding balance. When you choose to capitalize the interest, the amount outstanding on the reverse mortgage gradually increases as the interest accumulates on the loan.

A reverse mortgage seems like such a great idea to a lot of folks because you can get your hands on your equity even as you remain in your home. In fact, you can stay there until you die or choose to sell, at which point the reverse mortgage is repayable. It seems a little like having your cake and eating it too.

Assuming you die in residence, the house can either be sold to repay the outstanding balance or a regular mortgage can be used to finance the repayment to the reverse-mortgage company. If your house has more equity than you owe on the reverse mortgage, your estate gets the difference. If your house is worth less than you owe—either because you live a long life or because property values have fallen—that's not your problem. The reverse mortgage company is on the hook for any shortfall.

You have to be in your 60s to qualify for a reverse mortgage. Clearly this is a product targeted at an aging population. And the older you are, the more money you'll receive. That's because the older you are the less time your capitalized interest will compound, leaving more equity from which the reverse mortgage company can draw its repayment.

If you decide to reverse mortgage your home, having second thoughts can be extremely costly. While many contracts offer a cooling-off period during which you can change your mind, once that period expires, the contract is binding and you'll pay a hefty fee to break it. The cooling off period is just one of the features you should look at carefully before you sign on the dotted line. You should make sure you understand the covenants, or legal promises, you are making. Are you promising to keep the property in good repair? What'll happen if you don't? And how will the lender monitor the condition of your property? Once you're fully aware of the rules, you'll be able to decide whether or not you want to play the game.

You're a reverse mortgage candidate if the following apply to you:

- You're determined to stay put in your home for a long time.
- The idea of depleting your estate, perhaps completely, doesn't send shivers down your spine or make your kids consider having you committed.
- You're okay with the idea of your debt level going up, up, up.
- You're old enough to qualify. For once, older is better.
- You own your home outright.
- Your type of home qualifies. If you have a house, no problemo. Condos and duplexes are more complicated. Cooperatives and leaseholds don't stand a chance.

Because I am not a fan of reverse mortgages, I'm going to suggest you investigate other options before you take this step. If you think you need to use the equity in your home to provide an income, do the math on selling your home and either downsizing or renting so that you free up some of your capital. If you are determined to stay in your home, consider taking in a boarder or renting out a portion of the home. If you are determined to use a reverse mortgage, have your local lender run a comparison between the figures you get from your reverse mortgage company and using a home equity line of credit to access the equity in your home.

If at the end of the day you decide a reverse mortgage works for you, great. Just go into it with your eyes wide open.

LIVING ON LESS

Having figured out how much you're going to have to live on, you may come to the realization that it's not a wholehelluvalot. Whether you're forced to retire early, or you haven't saved enough and will have to learn to live on less, there are a few things you need to do to prepare to simplify your life and your spending.

People who don't make a lot of money love to say that they don't have enough money to make a budget; that's just an excuse. At no time is a budget more important than when you're living on a small income. It's also a good idea to build up a bit of a "slush" fund when you're living on a small income. Setting aside your change, or taking $2 a week out of your budget and setting it aside until you've accumulated $100 or so, means you'll have money available to take advantage of sales. If chicken goes on for 99¢ a pound, you can stock up.

Look for ways to significantly reduce your housing costs. Manage your mortgage down, so that your total housing costs represent 35% or less of your lower income. Downsizing or moving to a cheaper area or cheaper digs may work. Or you could go with a roommate. Or you could rent a room in your home to a student or to someone else who needs to cut costs. You have options. Look for them.

Having an emergency fund is extremely important when you have to live on less. Even a small emergency can be devastating to a budget that's so tight it squeaks. Make sure you have a stash of cash set aside just in case the worst happens so you aren't forced to use credit and incur interest costs when you can least afford it. If you have to sell some stuff to build this stash of cash, do it. Maybe you can take a part-time job until you've built up your safety net.

Just as important is ensuring that you know the difference between the things you need (must have to keep body and soul together) and want (would like to have.) I'm amazed at the people who can't tell the difference: the people who, despite not having any money in the bank, see no problem buying booze, take-out, and a new set of threads, putting it all on credit. Wake up! If you're living on limited resources, putting your Must-Haves at risk for dumb Wanna-Haves is not only short-sighted, it can be very painful because it leads to higher costs and lower cash flow.

It's virtually impossible to keep up with debt repayment if you're living on reduced income. Paying interest is hard when you have a good income. On a limited income, it's the difference between keeping the lights on or not. It doesn't matter what you can't have . . . what you must do without . . . don't go into debt. And if you have debt, you've got to find some way of ridding yourself of the burden. So, sure, working three jobs may suck for a while, but since you spent the money, it's now time to pay it back.

Learning to barter is another good strategy. What do you have or what can you do in exchange for something else you may need. Offer to weed a neighbour's veggie garden in exchange for a dozen zucchini. Offer to sit a friend's kids in exchange for a home-cooked meal. Give a foot rub to an elderly relative in exchange for stuff she no longer needs that you can sell second-hand.

Learning to do for yourself will also save you money. If you can repair what breaks, do your own maintenance, or make your own goods, you'll save gobs of money. While I had neither the tools nor the strength to remove a dead tree from my yard, I did have the skills to cook a lovely meal for the Sub-Hub (substitute husband) who did it for me. Ditto if you learn how to shop second-hand and develop other strategies for getting more for less. Find free fun. Learn to love your library. Make friends with people who also live frugally, and take their tips to heart.

You may not be able to live large on a small income, but that doesn't mean you can't have a good life. You need to get your priorities straight. And you need to stay focused on what's really important.

NINE WAYS TO COPE WITH NO SAVINGS

1. **Seventy is the new 65:** Staying in the workforce for a few more years means you can earn more money for the future and your retirement will be shorter.

2. **Keep working:** Cutting back to part-time employment rather than giving up work entirely means you'll need less of a stash of cash. It's been estimated that for every $5,000 a year that you earn, you'll need $100,000 less in retirement assets.

3. Start something new: Whether you love to sew, like to take photographs, or are an avid cook, can you turn what you love to do into a small business? You don't have to generate loads of money, just enough to cover your gap. And if you are doing something you love, that'll be way better than taking a crappy job that makes you hate to get out of bed.

4. Focus: Retirement savings must become your priority, period. Everything else has to play second fiddle. That may be tough to hear if you're trying to help your kids or deal with elderly parents. But if you don't start taking care of your own future, you'll be screwed. So it's time to get focused on what YOU need.

5. Cut to the bone: Dramatically cutting your expenses will help you save more. At the same time it will reduce the total amount you need to save because you'll get used to living on less. Do you still need that life insurance? How about cable? A home phone and a cellphone? A three-bedroom apartment?

6. Walk: Find a place to live within walking distance of stores and other amenities so you can eliminate the need for a vehicle.

7. Liquidate: Asset rich but cash poor? Consider turning your home into money by taking in roommates, selling and downsizing, or using a reverse mortgage. While I'm not a huge fan of reverse mortgages, they do serve a purpose for some people. Be very careful and do all your homework before you choose one of these as your option.

8. Grow your own: Do you live somewhere that you can grow a veggie garden, raise chickens, go fishing? Becoming more self-sufficient is not only satisfying, it's way cheaper.

9. Move: Relocating to a cheaper part of the country, or to a cheaper country, is also a possibility. While the majority of retirees want to age in place rather than start life over somewhere else, if that means having a really horrible last couple of decades, consider the adventure and excitement of trying something new. Loads of retirees choose to move, and some even go abroad to make their retirement funds go further. Try your new location on before you make a big commitment. Consider spending at least a few weeks in your destination area to make sure it's a good fit.

You can have what you want from your retirement assuming you haven't let your expectations get out of hand. If you've always lived simply, your retirement will likely be a continuation of your simplicity. If you've lived a buy, buy, buy life and find yourself in retirement with no money, you'll learn to embrace simplicity, or you'll be miserable. It's up to you.

Shift your attitude so that the things you need also become the things you want. Sadly, for many folks, the things we have are of far less value than the things we wish we had. If you are always taking the things you have for granted, it's too easy to focus on the things you have not, leaving you dissatisfied. But if you're determined to have a happy life, you'll see the joys in small things, appreciate what you do have, and focus on your blessings. You may not have a lot of money, but that doesn't mean your life can't be rich in love, in experiences, and in the small pleasures that truly do make a life worth living.

13

TIME TO WALK THE TALK

My girlfriends and I were chatting one day about the crap our kids did that blew our minds. We all have stories. I have the Alex-Kicked-the-Dog story. Marci had the Shelly-and-the-Banana story. And Dee told the story of her son, Mathew, and how he imported his sandbox into his room.

Mathew loved playing in the sandbox. When summer was almost over, Dee told Mathew that in a couple of weeks they'd be closing up the sandbox for the winter. Mathew seemed unfazed, much to Dee's surprise, since Mathew spent every waking moment in the sandbox with his trains. Oh, well, you just never know with kids.

Mathew shared a bedroom with his brother. Charlie's crib was in the corner of the room, and usually had one or two boxes stashed underneath. Over the next two weeks, each time Mathew left the sandbox, he took a bucket of sand out of the sandbox and piled it under Charlie's crib, behind the boxes.

Dee was almost crying with laughter when she pointed out that Mathew's plot only worked because she's the world's worst housekeeper. But as a working mom with three kids under eight, vacuuming wasn't top of the list. The little bugger moved almost his entire sandbox, one bucket at a time, into his room. And Dee found out when she went into the room early one morning to check on Charlie, only to find Mathew wedged under the crib, making train sounds.

We very seldom think about what can be accomplished with persistence and concerted effort. Sure, we know we should save. But saving $100 a month can seem like a futile effort. No one gets rich saving $100 a month, right?

Well, when did Mathew's pile of sand turn into a heap? Think about it. Sure, the first bucketful couldn't have been much fun. But this six-year-old had enough imagination and stick-to-it-ness to know that over time he'd have what he wanted. We'd do well to show the same patience and tenacity.

HAVE SOME PATIENCE

The only way to get a heap is to move a grain of sand into your pile. Little by little you will build your small contributions into a goodly sum of money. What is most important is that you are saving. Even if you start with just $25, $50, or $100 a month, that money is money you'll have later when you need it.

For most people, automating savings is the key to building a retirement nest egg. Begin by saving what you can and then slowly increase the amount as you go. Look for places to trim your expenses and move that money into your savings pool. The next time you get a raise, stash half the extra money you're earning in savings every month and watch your pile grow into a heap.

Remember, before you can have $10,000 you must save $1,000. Before you can save $1,000, you must save $100. Before you can save $100, you must save $10.

The thing about retirement planning—about saving in general—is that it's pretty straightforward. Don't spend all your money now and you'll have some for later when you may need it. How much you save depends on how much you want to have. Content with a simple lifestyle, sipping tea with mates over a game of chess? You can have that. Want to travel the world, play golf all summer, and leave the winter blahs behind come January? You can have that too. You'll have to work harder, spend less now, and save more for the future, but you can have it.

STRIVE FOR DOABLE, NOT PERFECTION

Planning for the future shouldn't be so onerous that you have to squeeze your budget as tight as a nun's knees. Instead, it should be about balancing today's needs with tomorrow's.

You may have to start small. If all you can muster is $25 a month, that's $25 a month more saved up and grown than if you did nothing at all. Over time, you'll get raises, find ways to shop smarter, get rid of debt. And that'll help you take that $25 a month to $50 a month. Then $100 a month. Soon you'll have worked saving for the future into your plan without feeling deprived and stressed out.

While it's tempting to take what The Spurts say to heart—hey, they're the guys in the know, right?—if all that causes you is a deepening sense of inadequacy you'll end up paralyzed by fear. I hate that! So I want you to close your ears to the doomsday chatter and focus on doing something. I don't care how small. Just save something. And keep saving something every month.

You can go into retirement with your eyes closed and your fingers crossed behind your back and hope for the best. Hey, if that's how you've done life so far, you're probably pretty good at it by now. But if you get there and find you're barely subsisting, don't whine.

Another alternative—some would say a better alternative—would be to take a realistic look at what you may need for retirement, how much you think you'll have, and what you can do to close the gap if there is one. And for heaven's sake, make sure you're debt free before you get there. Spending your limited resources paying for crap you bought on credit while you were still working should be the last thing you do.

Retirement planning should not be an exercise in frustration. It should be the conscious choice to make what you want of your future by setting aside the money you'll need to create your reality. If you set aside nothing—if you spend every red cent you make, and then some—you're making a choice. It won't be an easy one to live with later, but it is YOUR choice.

Choose instead to put a little effort into building up a retirement nest egg and you'll be surprised how easy it is, if you start early and do it consistently.

FEEL AND THEN DO

You now have all the practical steps for planning and moving into retirement. The only thing left is for you to create an image of what you want your retirement to feel like. Emotions motivate us. Fear makes us run away. Love makes us run towards. Contentment makes us sigh with pleasure. If you can create an image of how you want your retirement to feel, you'll find the motivation to make those feelings happen.

Feelings are magnetic. Positive feelings attract positivity into our lives. Be positive about what you can accomplish and you'll move towards your goals with far less friction. Not spending money on stuff you really don't need, and putting it towards creating the opportunity to realize those feelings you've imagined will be easier. And each time you measure how much closer you are to what is truly important to you, bathe in the good feelings, the sense of achievement, the joy of fulfillment.

When you are clear about what you really want, it's amazing how you'll move in the right direction automatically. And when you are clear on what you want to feel, you'll instinctively know when to say, "No thanks, that won't work for me" and when to say, "Yes, that's what I really want."

ACKNOWLEDGMENTS

Once again I'd like to send Curtis Russell, my agent and provocateur, a huge hug for insisting that I start writing books again. Hey, dude, thanks for being so persistent. And to my favouritest editor, Kate Cassaday, at HarperCollins—sweetie, I'd jump through hoops of fire for you.

The sales, marketing, and media folks at HarperCollins are fabulous. What a team! Glad to have you on my side.

And to all the people who keep asking me great questions, keep 'em coming.

INDEX

Page numbers in bold refer to material found in tables and charts.

A